MW01047548

# Understand... ...p... ...

# Understanding Computer Networks

By Apple Computer, Inc.

**Addison-Wesley Publishing Company**

Reading, Massachusetts ■ Menlo Park, California ■ New York
Don Mills, Ontario ■ Wokingham, England ■ Amsterdam ■ Bonn
Sydney ■ Singapore ■ Tokyo ■ Madrid ■ San Juan

Apple, the Apple logo, AppleTalk, AppleShare, LaserWriter, Macintosh, and IIGS are registered trademarks of Apple Computer, Inc.

EtherTalk and LocalTalk are trademarks of Apple Computer, Inc.

CompuServe is a registered service mark of CompuServe, Inc.

DIALOG is a registered trademark of DIALOG Information Services, Inc.

Dow Jones is a registered trademark of Dow Jones and Co., Inc.

Xerox is a registered trademark of Xerox Corporation.

IBM is a registered trademark of International Business Machines Corporation.

ITC Zapf Dingbats is a registered trademark of International Typeface Corporation.

LANSTAR is a registered trademark of Northern Telecom.

Linotronic is a trademark of Allied Corporation.

Microsoft is a registered trademark of Microsoft Corporation.

PageMaker is a registered trademark of Aldus Corporation.

POSTSCRIPT is a registered trademark of Adobe Systems Incorporated.

The Source is a registered service mark of Source Telecomputing Corporation.

Varityper is a registered trademark, and VT600 is a trademark, of AM International, Inc.

VT100 is a trademark of Digital Equipment Corporation.

Simultaneously published in the United States and Canada.

ISBN 0-201-19773-1

C D E F G H I J-KR-89

**Third printing, October 1989**

*Acknowledgments*

Written by Raymond Kristof
Designed by Lisa S. Mirski
Illustrations by Max Seabaugh (text) & Paul Woods (cover, chapter openings)

*Production Manager:* Patrick Ames
*Project Manager:* Rani Cochran
*Editor:* Paul Dreyfus
*Production Artist:* Graham Metcalfe
*Film and Print Supervisor:* Robin Kerns

*Technical Advisers:*
Henri Aebischer
Rich Andrews
Gursharan Sidhu

*Concept and guidance:* Paul Goode
*Faith and support:* Randy Battat

# Table of Contents

*Preface by Jean-Louis Gassée / xi*

## Introduction / 1

**Learning about computer networks / 3**

**Why network? / 3**
☐ Some network services and benefits / 4

**Let's get started / 5**

## 1 Overview of Computer Networks / 7

**What can a computer network connect? / 9**

**What is a computer network made of? / 10**
Network components / 10
Network architecture / 11

**Local and wide area networks / 12**
Local area networks / 12
Wide area networks / 12
Interconnecting networks / 12

**Network evolution: How did we get here? / 14**
Host-based computing / 14
Decentralized computing / 14
Peer-to-peer networking / 15

# 2 How Computer Networks Work / 17

**Names and addresses / 19**

**Transmission formats / 20**
What computer data looks like / 20
☐ The binary and decimal systems / 20
How computer data is transmitted / 21

**Protocols: the rules of the network / 22**
How protocols define network functions / 23
**A model for thinking about protocols / 24**
☐ The ISO/OSI model / 24

# 3 Making the Connection / 27

**Avoiding chaos: network access methods / 28**
Point-to-point networks / 28
Carrier sensing / 29
Token passing / 29

**Hooking up to a network / 30**
*Example:* AppleTalk connection options / 30
What the connection hardware does / 31
What the connection software does / 31

**Network media / 32**
Media characteristics / 32
   *Transmission speed / 32*
   *Maximum length / 32*
   *Shielding against interference / 32*

**Media type / 33**
Twisted-pair wiring / 33
Coaxial cable / 33
**Optical fiber / 33**
☐ Media comparison table / 34

**Transmission methods/ 35**

☐ Multiplexing / 35

**Network topologies / 36**

Bus topology / 36

Ring topology / 36

Star topology / 36

**Connecting networks together / 38**

☐ Devices that connect networks together / 38

    *Repeaters / 39*

    *Routers / 39*

    *Bridges / 39*

    *Gateways / 39*

## 4   Telecommunications in Computer Networks / 41

☐ Why we need modems / 43

**Wide area networks / 44**

Uses of wide area networks / 44

☐ Private uses of wide area networks / 45

☐ Commercial uses of wide area networks / 45

**Public data networks / 46**

Circuit switching and packet switching / 47

**Remote access to information / 48**

The role of communication software / 49

☐ Preventing unauthorized access / 49

## 5 Networking in Action / 51

**Network services / 53**
File servers / 53
Print servers / 54
Electronic mail / 54

**How network services are delivered / 55**

**Commercial services provided by computer networks / 56**
Information services / 56
Electronic mail / 56
Bulletin boards / 56
Electronic banking / 57
Credit checking / 57
Home shopping / 57
Airline ticketing / 57

## 6 Managing the Network / 59

**Network planning / 61**
Network needs analysis / 61
Market evaluation / 61
Preparation for growth / 61
The physical layout / 62

**Network management and administration / 63**
Network administration / 63

**What multiple computer vendors mean to networking / 64**

**Integrating network technologies / 65**

**Network standards / 66**
Vendor-developed standards / 66
Industry standards / 66
International standards / 66
☐ ISDN–A look at wide area networking to come / 67

**The future / 68**

*Epilogue* / 71

*Glossary* / 76

# Preface

Apple® Computer's approach to networking is colored by its roots, by its individual-centric as opposed to process-centric perspective of computing: It is our view that the computer primarily serves human beings and their creativity rather than their dispassionate processes, such as automated teller machines or industrial automation.

But in taking this view we strive to satisfy the needs of both the organization and the individual. The organization requires networking tools that are easy to install and manage, that preserve its existing investments in data and applications, that span diverse architectures. The individual wants services that reach over a wide expanse of wires, protocols, data structures—yet hide the irrelevant details. Apple's approach to networking in effect bridges these two cultures without asking either to compromise its values or assets.

To do this we need to recognize that wires, protocols, and network management, while good, necessary conditions for a computer network, are not good enough. For the computer network is far more than its material manifestation; in our view, the *how* of networking—its relative ease of use—is just as, if not more, important than the indispensable *what*.

Someday the computer network will become like the phone system: we won't worry about the underpinnings, we'll use it, we'll enjoy it and we'll pervert it (the mark of success), putting it to uses not foreseen by the inventors.

As we begin to move toward that "invisible" network, I hope you will enjoy this book as a friendly guide to a fascinating area of technology. Fascinating because the world is still ambivalent: will the network electrocute us or electrify us? Here at Apple, we have more than a little

bias toward the latter. And we would all feel very proud if you shared our bias, our excitement about the possibilities of the computer network when you finish this book. Then, together we can move closer to helping the network disappear, some day, like the Cheshire cat.

*Jean-Louis Gassée*

**Jean-Louis Gassée**
*President, Apple Products,*
*April 1989*

# Understanding Computer Networks

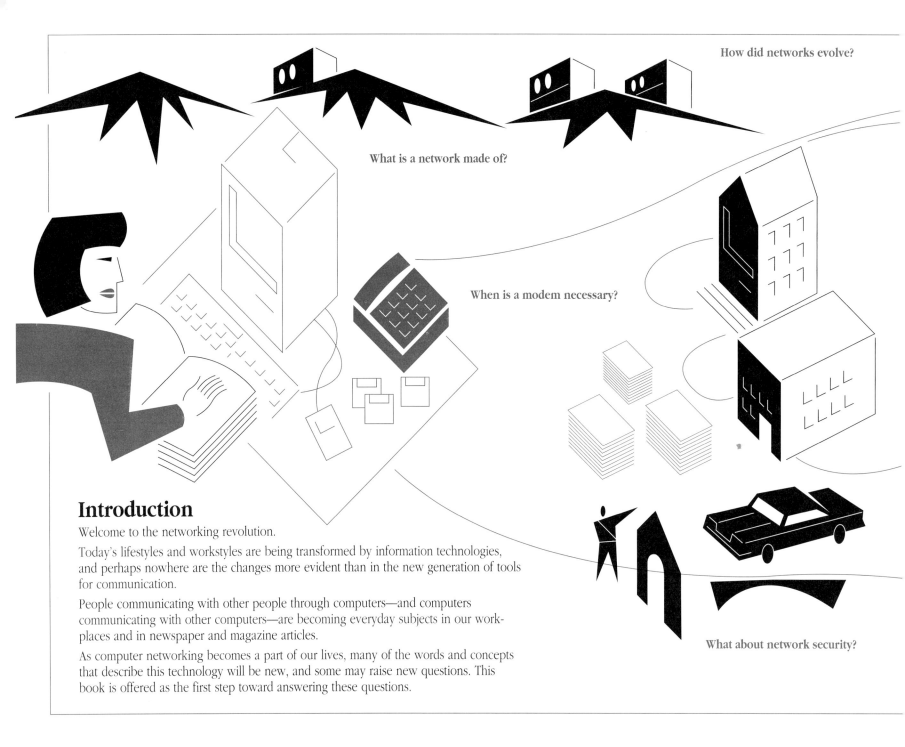

How did networks evolve?

What is a network made of?

When is a modem necessary?

What about network security?

# Introduction

Welcome to the networking revolution.

Today's lifestyles and workstyles are being transformed by information technologies, and perhaps nowhere are the changes more evident than in the new generation of tools for communication.

People communicating with other people through computers—and computers communicating with other computers—are becoming everyday subjects in our work-places and in newspaper and magazine articles.

As computer networking becomes a part of our lives, many of the words and concepts that describe this technology will be new, and some may raise new questions. This book is offered as the first step toward answering these questions.

What are network benefits?

How are networks put together?

What are the two main categories of networks?

Why does everything work together?

What about the future?

How is information sent across a network?

How is information sent to the right place?

Consider the three great leaps of civilization: agriculture, industry, and information. Each began with a revolutionary new tool: the plough, the machine, the computer. But none could fulfill its potential without the means to spread and integrate its revolutionary technology: irrigation, mass production, and—in the information age—the emergence of computer networks.

A single computer can contain only limited information. You can use this computer by itself to do only a limited number of things. But imagine all the different kinds of information available in computers in your workplace, in schools, libraries, and businesses of all kinds, and the many kinds of tasks people around you perform with these computers.

Networking is what happens when you connect your computer to these other computers and gain access to the wealth of information and services they provide. You can share information and work together with a colleague in the next office—or in another country—without leaving your desk.

## Learning about computer networks

If you use a computer in your work, it's likely that you are or will soon become a network user. Along with all the new information and services you'll have access to, you may be facing many new questions.

This book is for you if you want to learn

- what a computer network is
- how you can use it and what it can do for you
- how networks operate
- how networks differ from one another
- how different networks interact with one another

In the pages that follow, you'll see that computer networks observe straightforward and logical rules of operation that can be described in clear and simple language.

Whether your interest is personal or professional, whether you wish to become a network user or to evaluate systems for a purchase, the information in this book should help you to understand the basics of computer networking in a relatively short time.

## Why network?

What can a computer network do for you and your organization? What *is* a computer network?

There are many technical definitions of networks, but in practical terms, a computer network is a tool for communication which, at its best, makes distances and differences between computers invisible. Computer networks give people access to an ever-growing range of information resources and services.

The next time you use your automated bank teller card, remember that you're using a computer network. Each time you make an airline reservation, ask a telephone operator for a number, or have your groceries scanned at the supermarket, you're using services that are made possible by computer networks.

In workplaces like your own, the objective is the same: to *access* information on other computers and to *exchange* information with other network users. Networks help people work faster and smarter by making the information they need available when they need it, where they need it.

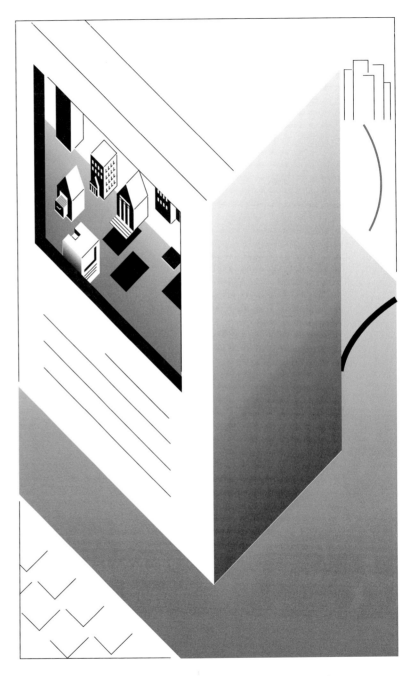

# Some network services and benefits

**Sharing information**

You and other network users can have access to the same information; for example, you can collaborate electronically on a project report with others in your work group—each of you performing a part of the task on your own personal computer.

**Accessing remote information**

You can use your personal computer to check stock prices or airline schedules through a public information service, or to dial up your own company's databases for information about, for example, warehouse inventory or quarterly sales.

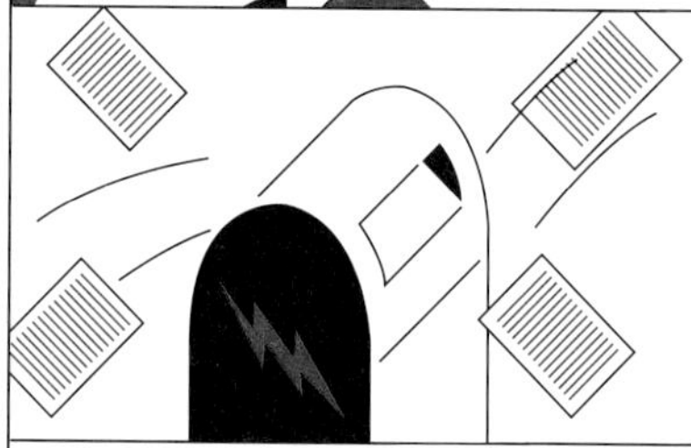

**Communicating with others**

You can exchange messages with computer users in your local work group or around the world by means of electronic mailboxes, a quick and paperless form of communication.

**Sharing applications**

You and several other users can have access to the same application software; for example, everyone in your work group can upgrade to the newest version of a database program by accessing a shared storage disk.

**Sharing network resources**

Networks allow users to share connected devices. For example, with a network device called a print server, you can send files to a network printer and regain immediate use of your computer for other tasks; the server then handles print requests in the order received.

# Let's get started

As we enter the 1990s, the information age has been in progress for some time, and its impact has come to be felt in nearly every aspect of society. But only now—as millions of computers are connected to networks, and these computer networks, in turn, are spanning the globe through interconnected telephone and satellite systems—has it become clear that networking is the catalyst through which we can gain the full benefits of the information age.

How can hooking up to a network change so many things? What is the network's secret? In the following chapters, you'll learn about the components and systems of rules and standards that make networking possible, and the numerous ways that network services are changing how we work and live.

First, some definitions are in order. Once these basic concepts have been explained, you'll see how they work as building blocks toward easily understanding computer networks.

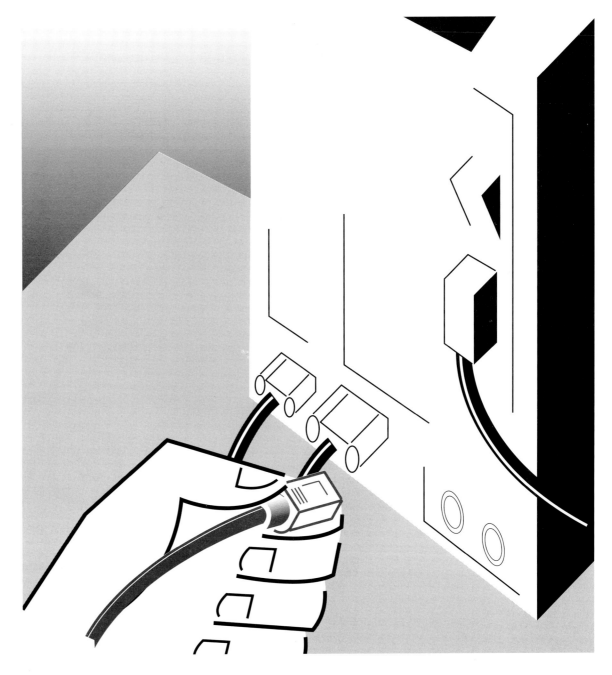

# 1 / Overview of Computer Networks

The term *network* suggests a collection of related things or people that are somehow interconnected. The global telephone network is one familiar example. In a *computer network,* the interconnected parts are computers and other devices that communicate with each other. The network is the means by which they can be connected to one another and exchange information.

Simply put, a computer network is a tool for communication. Like all tools, it helps people to perform some kind of task—or several tasks. As you'll soon see, computer networks come in a multitude of forms and can be applied to many tasks.

A computer network is created whenever one computer is connected to other computers and/or devices such as printers or display terminals in a way that allows users to share information or computing resources.

A computer network may connect as few as two computers or as many as thousands or even millions.

**This is a network.**  ▶

The computers and printer are connected by a network cable that can also connect other computers, allowing the printer to be shared by other computer users.

**This is not a network.**  ▶

The computer and the printer are joined by a directly connected cable, so the printer cannot be shared by other computer users.

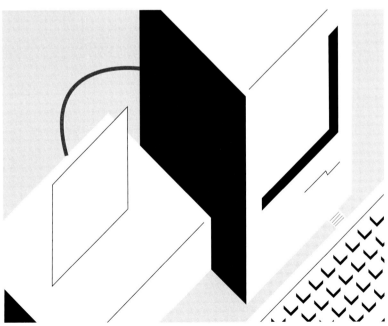

## What can a computer network connect?

**Personal computers.** A primary use of networks is to let users communicate with each other and access remote services through their personal computers.

**Shared resources.** Many computer resources, such as high-speed printers, can be made more cost-efficient if multiple users are allowed to share them.

**Network servers.** Some important capabilities of computer networks, like information sharing and electronic mail, may be delivered by network servers—computers with special software that provides those services.

**Minicomputers and mainframe computers.** Interconnected computers of varying types and sizes serve a broad range of functions on networks, such as centralized data base management, file service, and network control.

**Other networks.** Special devices can connect together two or more computer networks, allowing users to gain access to information and services on other—in many cases distant—networks.

# What is a computer network made of?

A computer network can best be described in terms of its *components* and its *architecture*.

- **Components** are all of the network's functional parts.
- **Architecture** determines how the network's components work together.

## Network components

A computer network is made up of the following components:

- **Hardware**
  Computers
  Shared printers and servers
  Media
  Connection devices
- **Software**
  User applications
  Network control software

**Network hardware** includes computers and shared devices (such as printers) that are connected to the network, as well as media and connection devices.

**Network software** consists of the applications that network users see—such as electronic mail or file sharing software—and the underlying control software that allows network components to work together.

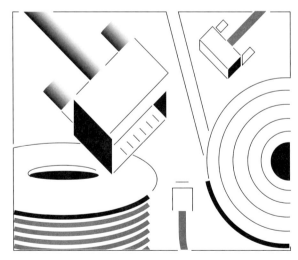

**Network media** refers to the physical conductors—such as electrical cables or optical fibers—through which information is transmitted.

**Connection devices** connect computers and media together; examples are a special circuit board that enables a computer to transmit information, or a bridging device that interconnects two networks.

## Network architecture

The architecture of a computer network is the design plan of how the network's components work together. It is what distinguishes one network from another.

Two different computer networks can have many *components* in common, but their *architecture* makes them different. For example, two networks can use the same kinds of cables and connectors, but still have very different architectures.

The architecture of a computer network has two main aspects:

■ **Communication protocols** are the rules that govern interaction between devices on a network. Protocols determine—among many other things—how devices can exchange information, in what form the information is transmitted, and how multiple devices can send information on the same cable in an orderly way.

■ **Topology** defines how the network's components are arranged in relation to each other. A network's topology is the physical layout of the network.

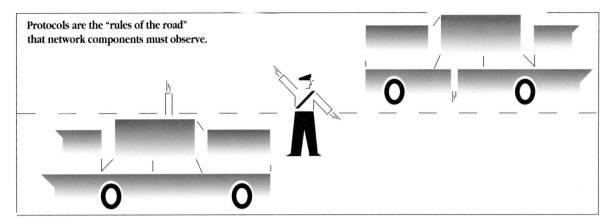

Protocols are the "rules of the road" that network components must observe.

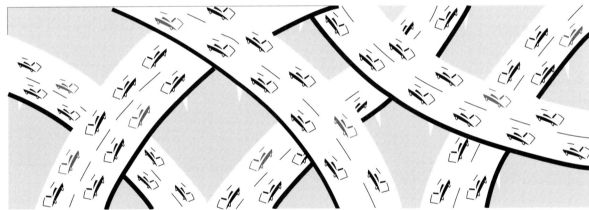

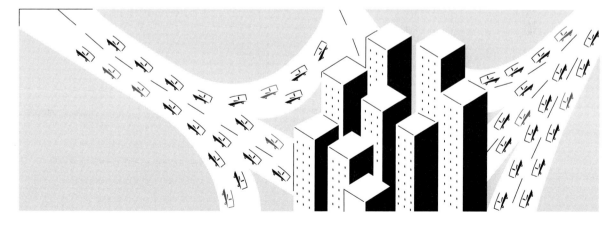

# Local and wide area networks

Computer networks can be designed in many different ways, depending on their physical environment—office, factory, college campus—and on the way they are used; for example, connecting a few personal computers to a printer and file server, or many thousand automated tellers to a distant bank computer.

Two categories that are often used to describe computer networks are **local area network** and **wide area network.** These descriptions are also referred to by the acronyms LAN and WAN.

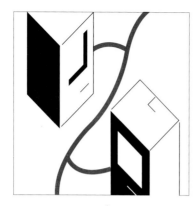

## Local area networks

A local area network is made up of computers and shared devices that are physically connected together in a limited area—generally a single building or office site.

A LAN might involve just a handful of users or as many as hundreds or thousands. The transmission speed of a LAN is relatively high, and, typically, the network cables and connection equipment are owned by the organization using the network.

For example, a local area network might serve a corporate publications department consisting of writers, artists, and editors collaborating on projects, all working in the same site. The LAN can allow these users to exchange messages and documents, and to print files and artwork on shared network printers.

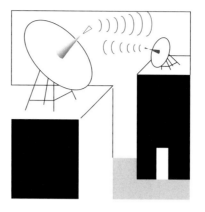

## Wide area networks

A wide area network consists of computers that are generally far apart and that may use telephone, satellite, or other long-distance connections to communicate with each other.

In contrast with a LAN, the connections in a WAN are often made over equipment that is not owned by the user's organization. The WAN services might be provided by a telephone company or other seller of telecommunication services.

For example, a wide area network might be used by a bank's central computer system connected to many branch offices nationally. Such a system continuously receives records of customer transactions from remote sites, and updates customer files accordingly.

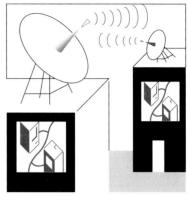

## Interconnecting networks

Often, two or more networks are connected to each other, forming an **internet.** An organization might have a large local area network installed at its headquarters and smaller networks in several field offices, and might keep the users of these local networks in touch with each other through a wide area network.

An internet may consist of a group of local area networks, or a combination of local and wide area networks.

Networks can be connected to each other through a variety of special connection devices, including modems, bridges, routers, and gateways. These devices are discussed in Chapters 3 and 4.

# Network evolution: How did we get here?

Large mainframe computers with multiple terminals have been around for many years. But if these multi-user computers themselves allow people to access information and share resources, why have networks of personal computers now become so popular?

The answer reveals the force driving the network revolution: people want *personal* control of their computing power—at their own desks—in addition to access to information.

## Host-based computing

Connecting many terminals to a central mainframe, or "host-based" computing, requires all users to share one computer. The host does all the computing while little storage or processing capabilities are available at users' terminals. In contrast, networks of personal computers enable individual users to have the processing power, autonomy, and flexibility afforded by a computer on their own desktop.

Host-based computing is still a common method of resource sharing in environments where large data bases must be accessed by multiple users. This was the earliest form of resource sharing, because computers were large and extremely expensive, while terminals were small and less expensive—an arrangement that naturally led to environments with one host and multiple terminals.

## Decentralized computing

The reduction in size and cost of computers in the 1960s and 1970s made it possible to install computers closer to users and sources of data. Rather than one very large, central data processing system on which all departments in a company depended, smaller computers were purchased to do departmental data processing.

For example, a company might have one minicomputer handling order-entry and invoicing, another performing sales and marketing functions, and a mainframe computer handling payroll and accounting.

Decentralized computing only worked, of course, if the billing computer could transmit its figures to the accounting system, the marketing system could acquire its customer lists from the mainframe, the mainframe could acquire inventory data from the order-entry system, and so on.

For a long time, such exchanges were typically handled by physically carrying information on magnetic tapes from computer to computer. This procedure was awkward and time consuming, and particularly inefficient over long distances. It became increasingly clear that direct communication between computers was required.

The spread of computer networking—connection and communication between independent computer systems—was thus first fueled by mainframes and mini-computers.

## Peer-to-peer networking

Today, the picture is changing rapidly. The overwhelming trend is toward *peer-to-peer* connections, in which individual users have equal access to network resources without being reliant on mainframe control of those resources. Users want independent processing power on their own desktops, control over their own files and applications, and instant access to worlds of shared information resources and services.

Peer-to-peer networking not only enhances each user's power and productivity but has the added benefit that no central host system can fail and suddenly disable all users. While some applications, such as airline reservations, will still depend on centralized databases for the foreseeable future, an increasing proportion of overall business productivity relies on tools for *personal* productivity and communication.

As computers have grown smaller, less expensive, and more widely distributed in organizations, networking has evolved as the force that binds together the computing community.

# 2 / How Computer Networks Work

Now that we've seen the individual parts that make up a computer network, let's take a closer look at what's really happening behind the scenes when computers communicate. What makes the network work?

We'll begin by considering some basic concepts that are common to sending things from place to place—whether on a network or in the world at large—like addressing and packaging. Then we'll see how these concepts apply to the many interactions involved in moving information around the network.

Finally, we'll look closely at the master plans behind these interactions—the framework of protocols, or rules, that explicitly dictate how network devices must interact with one another.

# Names and addresses

Since networks can have many different sizes and shapes, some organizing scheme must exist to keep track of network devices so that the information you transmit finds its destination. That scheme is called **addressing.** The way a network performs addressing is one of the functions defined by the network's protocols.

Addressing is the fundamental scheme by which all networks manage the transfer of information. When network software performs a task like sending a file to a printer or transmitting a mail message between users, the software requires the addresses of both the sender and destination.

Every device that might be the target of a transmission on the network—such as a computer or a printer—is called a **node** and each node has an address. This address is used to identify the node, in the same way that addresses of homes or businesses identify their location.

A node's address contains a **node number** and may also identify the network on which the node is connected.

As a network user, you may never need to know or use a node's address. When using the AppleTalk® network system, for example, you are presented with only the **names** of available network services. When you select the name of a service you wish to use, such as a file server, AppleTalk network software translates this name into a network address.

The role of network software is to mask from users the operating details of procedures such as addressing, and to present users with only the information they need.

# Protocols: the rules of the network

The term *protocol* is best known in the context of diplomacy. A protocol is a code of interaction for a specific situation, in which both parties behave and respond in a prescribed manner. *Network protocols* are the rules that network devices must follow to successfully interact with one another.

Understanding protocols is central to understanding networks because people so often talk about networks in terms of their protocols. For example, an article may cite the many "TCP/IP networks" on college campuses, even though TCP/IP describes only a set of protocols—not a physical network. Likewise, the term "AppleTalk network" could refer to any network that uses AppleTalk protocols.

People discuss networks in terms of their protocols because protocols govern nearly everything a computer network does. Protocols define the actual steps that any device or program must take to communicate with another device or program on the network.

Returning to the example of diplomatic protocols, it's known that communication takes place

A network is said to *use* protocols, or *observe* protocols, but protocols aren't physically tangible parts of the network.

One common source of confusion is that people talk about protocols "doing" a network task or "controlling" some aspect of communication, and imply that protocols are active entities on a network. This is incorrect.

When you read, for example, that some networking protocol "manages interactions between computers and printers," this means that the protocol was written to *specify* how those devices communicate. The protocol itself is not a thing that resides on the network and manages other things on the network.

Protocol rules are built into networking software, and network devices observe protocols each time they perform a task, such as transmitting a document from one computer to another.

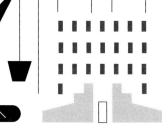

**A protocol is like a blueprint: It guides the construction but does not take part in it.**

horizontally among diplomats of equal status: one head of state may be directly addressed by another, but not by a low-level diplomat. However, there are several layers of ministers and ambassadors beneath these heads of state who take part in making their communication possible, each addressing a counterpart at his or her own level. An analogous hierarchy of protocols governs communication on a computer network: when two users' applications communicate, each has

an underlying framework of controlling software that makes their dialog possible.

In any network architecture, there must exist protocols that define three general classes of functions:

■ **Application services** are the highest level network functions. They enable an application program to communicate with an equivalent program on another computer.

■ **Transport services** are lower-level network functions, which manage addressing and other transmission control tasks.

■ **Connection services** are the lowest-level network functions. These govern the actual, physical transmission from one computer's memory onto the network, and then into the destination computer.

This progression of events is detailed in the following sections.

## How protocols define network functions

To illustrate the kinds of behaviors that are prescribed by protocols, consider the things that a device on a network might do while performing a typical task like sending an electronic mail message. (Note that in the adjoining examples, these procedures are simplified, showing only some of the protocol interactions involved, and that the order of events varies in different programs.)

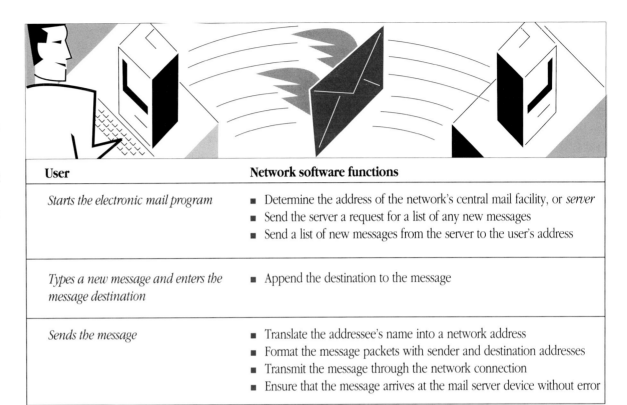

| User | Network software functions |
|---|---|
| *Starts the electronic mail program* | ■ Determine the address of the network's central mail facility, or *server*<br>■ Send the server a request for a list of any new messages<br>■ Send a list of new messages from the server to the user's address |
| *Types a new message and enters the message destination* | ■ Append the destination to the message |
| *Sends the message* | ■ Translate the addressee's name into a network address<br>■ Format the message packets with sender and destination addresses<br>■ Transmit the message through the network connection<br>■ Ensure that the message arrives at the mail server device without error |

The example above includes some of the more visible activities governed by protocols. To perform each of these tasks, additional protocols are required to do things like

■ control access to the network

■ identify the user's address to the server

■ establish a communication session between the devices

■ make sure the information is transmitted in the appropriate format.

As you can see, different protocols deal with tasks that occur at different levels of network operations: some are concerned with acquiring commands from the user application, as in the preceding electronic mail example, others with making sure the devices are aware of each other and responding properly, and still others with controlling connection to the network and moving data between devices.

For this reason, network protocols are generally referred to in terms of the levels, or *layers,* of activity they perform. The International Standards Organization (ISO) has published a model for layered network protocols that has become widely used for describing and comparing different network protocol architectures.

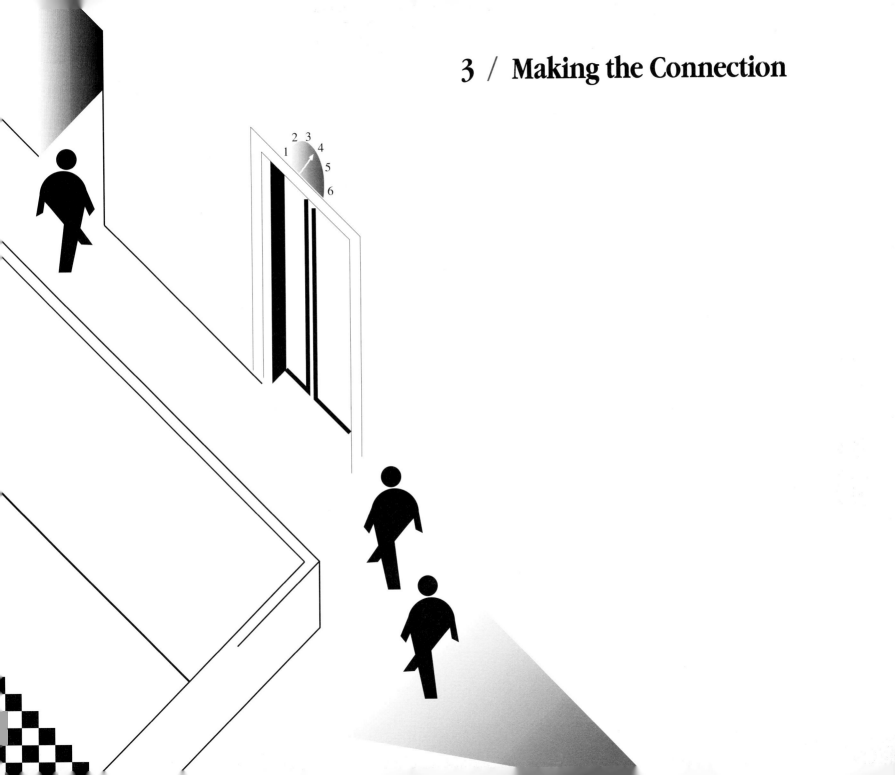

L et's turn our attention outward now and follow information as it leaves the computer. In this chapter, we'll first see how several computers or network devices can share the same medium. Then, we'll look at what's involved in physically hooking up to a network, consider diverse network cable types and other transmission media, and look at the most common kinds of topologies, or ways of laying out a network.

## Avoiding chaos: network access methods

Often, especially in local area networks, many devices transmit information on the same network cable. How can these devices share the cable without having their transmissions jumbled together? If they take turns, how do they know when to transmit, and for how long?

**Access methods**—the way a network manages access by multiple devices—observe protocols that are part of the data link layer in the protocol hierarchy. Data link protocols control the timing and coordination of the physical transmission.

### Point-to-point networks

Note that the access methods described here apply only to networks that *share* transmission media. While this includes all the most common computer networks, some networks can be designed in a *point-to-point* arrangement having a single, dedicated cable between any two communicating devices.

## Carrier sensing

One common method of controlling access to network media is called **carrier sensing.** This method is often referred to by the acronym CSMA, which stands for *carrier sense, multiple access.* The LocalTalk™ cable system from Apple Computer is one of many network types using the CSMA access method.

The "carrier" is the signal on the cable. In a network using CSMA, each device checks the cable before transmitting and if it senses a carrier—indicating that the cable is in use—it must back off and try again later. (The electrical signals involved occur at rates of thousands or even millions of pulses per second.)

In spite of these precautions, two devices could check the cable at precisely the same time, find no carrier, and begin to transmit, causing their transmissions to collide. To handle this situation, the access protocol often specifies a method of detecting collisions and retransmitting the data if a collision has occurred. This scheme is called CSMA/CD, for carrier sense, multiple access, with *collision detection.*

A *collision avoidance* scheme (CSMA/CA) is also used, in which collisions are not physically detected but their occurrence can be inferred based on non-response, elapsed time

intervals, and other means. Again, after a suitable wait (only microseconds), data that is presumed lost is retransmitted.

## Token passing

An alternative to giving each node free access to the network at any time is to give each node its own turn at gaining access to the cable. This is accomplished by an access method called **token passing.**

In the token passing method, a special sequence of bits representing the "token" is passed around the cable from node to node.

When a node is holding the token, it has sole access to the cable and can transmit freely without risk of collision.

If a node has data to transmit, it can take its turn; otherwise, it allows the token to pass. A limit on the amount of time allowed to each node prevents the cable from being

monopolized by a long transmission from any one node.

The token may be passed in a continuous sequence from each node to the node immediately next to it, or in a nonsequential order that is determined by network software.

# Hooking up to a network

What does it take to connect a computer to a network? Could just any computer become part of a network? The answers depend on the sort of network to which you're hooking up your computer.

In general, there are three ways that a computer can be connected to a network:

- via *built-in* circuitry and special software in the computer. Some computers, such as the Apple Macintosh®, are equipped with a network connector—called a network port—that allows a network cable to be plugged directly into the computer.

- via *added-in* connection hardware and software. In many cases, network connection circuitry can be installed inside the computer's housing in the form of a plug-in circuit board. Such a board generally includes a network port to connect the network cable.

- via **modem.** A modem is a device that lets you hook up to a remote computer or network through a telephone line. Hooking up to a remote network, like connecting to a local network, requires special software and circuitry. The modem provides the necessary circuitry, and the software that manages the connection may be in the local computer, a remote computer, or both. Modems and telecommunications are discussed further in the next chapter.

Nearly all computers being built today provide for one or more of these options, because using network services is becoming an indispensable part of computing.

---

*Example:* **AppleTalk connection options**

The AppleTalk network options for connecting computers to different cable systems illustrate the different connection types:

**Built-in connection:** The LocalTalk cable system was originally designed for Macintosh computers and LaserWriter® printers. The necessary software, circuitry, and ports are built in so that the computer and printer can be connected directly to a network.

**Added-in connection:** Apple also designed connection hardware and software that would allow other computers, like the Apple® IIe and the IBM PC, to be connected to LocalTalk cables. These connections are based on circuit boards that a user can simply plug into a slot inside the computer, and accompanying software with which to access network services.

A computer can have *both* built-in and added-in connections. For example, a Macintosh computer might be connected to LocalTalk as well as to a different kind of cable, such as Ethernet (through added-in circuitry), and select services alternatively from one or the other.

## What the connection hardware does

The connection device that transmits and receives packets between the computer and the network medium is called a **transceiver.** This device may be built into the computer, added in on a circuit board, or in some cases connected as an external unit.

The transceiver performs the lowest-level protocol functions—those that occur at the physical layer. It is responsible for controlling the signal that is sent out onto the network cable, as well as receiving the incoming signal. Since the nature of a data signal—its speed, voltage, and so on—is different when it's traveling inside a computer's memory than when it's on a network cable, the transceiver is needed to convert the signal from one form to the other.

In addition, the connection hardware may also filter out unwanted data signals and electrical noise, check for activity on the medium before transmitting, and synchronize the timing of the transmission as needed by the network.

## What the connection software does

Network connection software is sometimes referred to as a *network driver.* This driver manages the network access methods—like carrier sensing or token passing—and prepares the data for transmission on the network cable.

Network connection software may be built into the computer's operating system, may reside in special network control chips (called "firmware"), or may be installed separately with an added-in circuit board. This software implements network protocols that perform the "lowest-level" tasks of networking. (If you recall the hierarchy of network protocols from the last chapter, functions that deal with the user's applications are *higher*-level, and functions that manage network connections are *lower*-level.)

# Network media

The cables and other carriers of a network's transmission signals are called **media.**

In many ways, network media are like the electrical cables connected to your desk lamp or stereo speakers, but since computer networks need to transmit signals at very high levels of speed and reliability, they use special cables that best meet those needs.

While the more technical aspects of media are beyond the scope of this book, the pages that follow describe the most common types of network media in use and suggest why you might choose one or the other. Although the choice of network media has often been dictated by the network vendor you select, network systems, such as AppleTalk, are increasingly offering more than one cable option.

## Media characteristics

Network media can be described in terms of three main characteristics:

- transmission speed
- maximum length
- shielding against interference

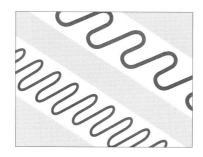

### *Transmission speed*

While a given network's capacity for moving data is governed by the network's design and transmission method, the transmission *medium* it uses may also limit transmission speed. Physical properties of different media types make them suitable for higher or lower rates of data throughput, as shown by the media comparison table on page 34.

In practical use, the transmission speed of a network is further modified by the the degree of reliability required of the network. Signal interference and other factors can reduce media reliability, requiring transmission to be limited to slower speeds. (For this reason, public telephone lines used for data, for example, have relatively low transmission speed limits.)

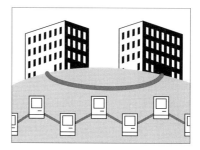

### *Maximum length*

The signal transmitted by network devices cannot travel indefinitely. After a given distance, the signal begins to weaken, lose integrity, and experience severe distortion.

A given network media type may have a prescribed maximum length between devices (or segment length), as well as an overall maximum network length.

These distances can be augmented in a number of ways, by using devices called repeaters and bridges that extend cable length, or by joining multiple networks into internets, as described later in this chapter.

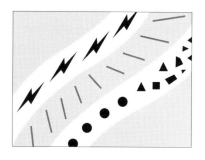

### *Shielding against interference*

When you hear static, hissing, or distortion in your telephone or radio receiver, the cause is often some form of electromagnetic interference in the signal from other signals in or near its path. This may be only a minor annoyance during a phone call, but may have serious consequences when the integrity of your data is at stake.

You can partially protect transmissions by locating network cables away from potential sources of interference, but isolating cables from each other is becoming increasingly difficult as electronic equipment proliferates throughout most offices.

Network cables are available with varying forms of shielding that can lessen the signal's sensitivity to outside interference. In addition, the network's signalling method and speed can also affect the cable's sensitivity to interference.

# Media Type

The following three types of cable are the most commonly encountered in computer networks, but are by no means the only ones available. Networks can also transmit signals via infrared light waves—often used to transmit between buildings when installing direct cables is impractical—and microwave signalling, which is a form employed in long-distance network transmissions by satellite.

■ **Twisted-pair wiring** is a popular, low-cost network cable type also used for standard telephone wiring. Its characteristics make it ideal for lower speed networks with segments of moderate length, although higher-speed twisted-pair networks are becoming available and are likely to gain prominence.

Twisted-pair wiring is made up of two wires that are twisted around each other so that external interference is equal in the two wires, minimizing its effect. Each wire is insulated, and the pair is usually covered by an overall casing. Common phone-grade twisted-pair wiring is generally not provided with any special shielding against interference, while some networks use shielded twisted-pair wiring.

■ **Coaxial cable** typically has higher performance specifications than twisted-pair wiring. It is the conductor of choice for use in higher-speed networks like Ethernet because of its high bandwidth and low sensitivity to electrical interference. Coaxial cable can be used in computer networks at speeds of up to 16 million bits per second or more.

You may be familiar with coaxial cable because it is used in homes to install community antenna television (CATV), or "cable TV." It consists of a central conductor wire surrounded by a layer of insulation, a conductive mesh sleeve, and an outer shielded insulator.

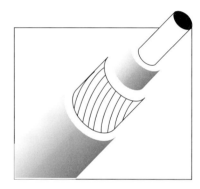

■ **Optical fiber** is a transmission medium using *light* rather than an electric current to transmit a signal. It requires a light source at the transmitting end and a detector at the receiving end, and transmits an extremely high-speed signal through fine fibers made of glass or glass-like synthetics. The light is generated by a laser at speeds of up to a billion or more pulses per second.

Optical fiber networks are highly effective for long-distance, high-throughput connection tasks due to the medium's speed and extremely high immunity to interference.

At present, the cost and complexity of installing a light source and detector make fiber optics an expensive solution for desktop-to-desktop transmission. However, developments in low-cost optical fiber transceivers will make fiber optic local area networks commonplace in the future.

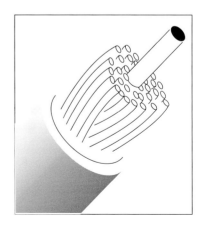

The adjoining table compares the characteristics of the three principal types of network media. These ratings are not absolute but relative to the other listed media types. The appropriateness of any media type for a network depends on the environment in which it will be used—the network size, level of use, physical conditions, and overall investment in network products—as well as the kinds of applications for which the network will be used. Cable with relatively low-performance specifications may be more than adequate for small networks with few concurrent users.

Continuing developments in media technologies are also blurring the boundaries between ratings for different media. High-speed transmission methods for twisted-pair wiring are now becoming available, for example, enabling this media type to be used for 10–megabit per second Ethernet transmissions. Likewise, the next generation of transceivers for fiber optic networks may make installing this media type relatively simple.

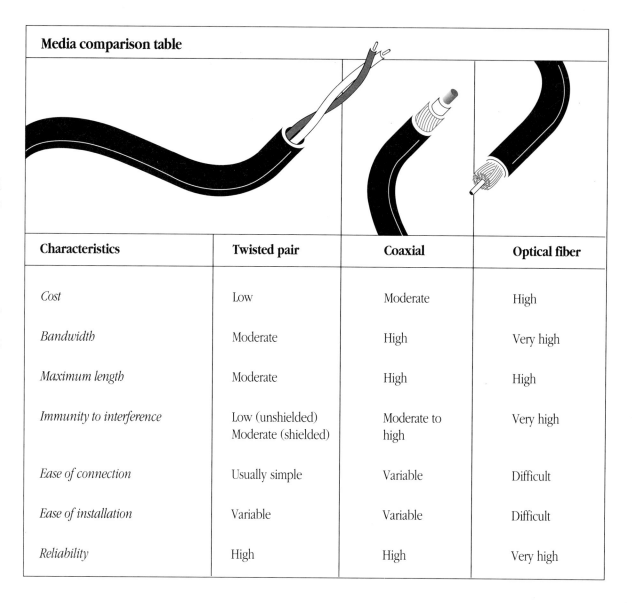

**Media comparison table**

| Characteristics | Twisted pair | Coaxial | Optical fiber |
|---|---|---|---|
| *Cost* | Low | Moderate | High |
| *Bandwidth* | Moderate | High | Very high |
| *Maximum length* | Moderate | High | High |
| *Immunity to interference* | Low (unshielded) Moderate (shielded) | Moderate to high | Very high |
| *Ease of connection* | Usually simple | Variable | Difficult |
| *Ease of installation* | Variable | Variable | Difficult |
| *Reliability* | High | High | Very high |

# Transmission methods

A network that transmits multiple signals at once by subdividing its transmission medium into channels is said to be using the **broadband** transmission method, while a network that transmits all signals through a single channel, one at a time, is using the **baseband** method.

Like your radio's band—the range of transmission frequencies used for broadcasting—a network's transmission band can be subdivided into separate channels, each carrying information from a different source. A network's range of transmission frequencies is called its **bandwidth.** The higher the bandwidth, the higher the network's potential throughput.

For example, a network could transmit either *one* signal at the maximum specified bandwidth, or several *different* signals simultaneously on different channels, each using a portion of the available bandwidth—not separate physical cables, but sections of the total range of transmission frequencies.

Broadband transmission—dividing a network's bandwidth into channels—is often used to send signals of different kinds simultaneously, such as voice and data. Since this method requires converting the digital signal into a different form, it adds complexity and cost to network components. Most local area computer networks use the baseband method. Although this throughput is measured in bits per second, the term bandwidth is still often used in reference to network throughput..

Bandwidth is a fundamental property of networks because the rate of throughput directly affects how fast the network responds to users: at times of heavy use, a network with a lower bandwidth will cause users to wait longer for their transmissions than one with a higher bandwidth.

Raw speed alone, however, is only one of many factors determining network performance. Others include how efficiently the network software has been designed and how efficiently the physical network itself is laid out.

## Multiplexing

The subdivision of a transmission medium to allow it to carry multiple signals is called **multiplexing.**

When two or more signals are transmitted simultaneously using different portions of the medium's frequency range (broadband transmission) this method of subdivision is called *frequency division multiplexing*.

When two or more signals are transmitted by alternating between the signals from each source, giving each a limited time in which to transmit, the method of subdivision is called *time division multiplexing*.

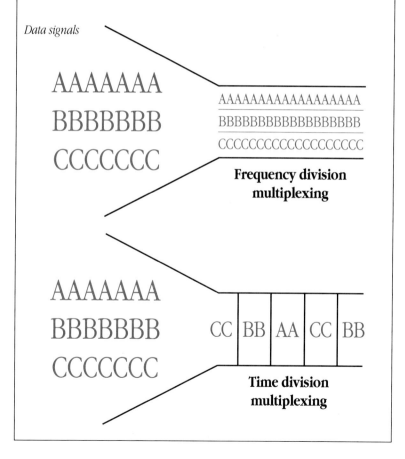

*Data signals*

AAAAAAA
BBBBBBB
CCCCCCC

AAAAAAAAAAAAAAAAAA
BBBBBBBBBBBBBBBBBB
CCCCCCCCCCCCCCCCCC

**Frequency division multiplexing**

AAAAAAA
BBBBBBB
CCCCCCC

CC | BB | AA | CC | BB

**Time division multiplexing**

# Network topologies

**Topology** is more than just the layout of a computer network. It is the part of network architecture that prescribes how you may arrange network devices relative to one another, and influences what methods they can use to access the network and transmit information to each other.

There are many possible topologies, as well as possible combinations of these. Although the choice of a network topology has traditionally been governed by the network manufacturer, topology is becoming increasingly uncoupled from the network selection process, as network systems are evolving to support multiple topologies.

The three most common network topologies for local area networks are described here.

## Bus topology

A bus network has a linear topology in which computers and other network devices are attached along the network cable from end to end. A bus network always has two distinct ends rather than a continuous loop of cable. Devices are connected along the length of this bus by connectors called *cable taps,* or by *drop cables* that extend from the device to the bus.

Transmissions on a bus are broadcast along the entire length of the cable. The receiving device whose address matches the destination address of any packet accepts and reads the packet, while the others simply ignore it.

The bus is a highly effective and reliable network configuration because no central controlling device is required, so no central failure can bring down the whole network (although a disconnection along the main cable will interrupt the network). In addition, adding and removing computers is less disruptive on a bus network than in any other topology.

## Ring topology

In a ring network layout, all network devices are connected in a daisy chain, forming a closed loop. Each packet is sent around the ring from node to node until it reaches its destination. At each stop, the node reads the packet's destination address. If the receiving node is the intended destination, it intercepts the packet; if not, the packet is sent on to the next node in the ring.

As in a bus network, each node is expected to recognize its own address on packets, but in a ring network, the data is passed from node to node rather than being broadcast on the entire cable. Since each segment of cable between nodes is an independent part of the journey around the ring, only one node at a time will be transmitting on any given segment.

## Star topology

A star network is laid out so that all of its nodes radiate from a central controlling node. This controller can be a computer running special software or a dedicated routing device—called a *switch.* The controlling node is connected to each network node through a dedicated channel, so it can explicitly direct a transmission to any one node rather than broadcast it to the entire network.

The protocol for routing information in a star network provides for the central controller to know the address of each node and the channel through which it is connected. The controller is then responsible for reading the destination address of each packet and routing it through the appropriate channel.

Networks that use telephone wiring as their media—an increasingly popular option—are generally star networks because wires radiate out to users' telephones from central control boxes.

**Bus topology** ▶

A layout scheme in which devices on a network are connected along the length of a main cable, or *bus*, rather than in a daisy chain or a loop.

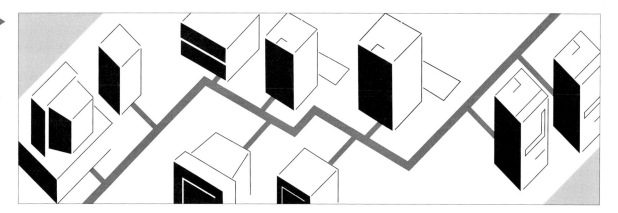

**Ring topology** ▶

A layout scheme in which network devices are connected by the physical medium in a closed loop.

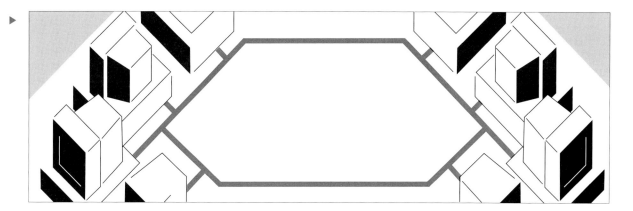

**Star topology** ▶

A layout scheme in which network devices are arranged so that all are connected to a central controlling device.

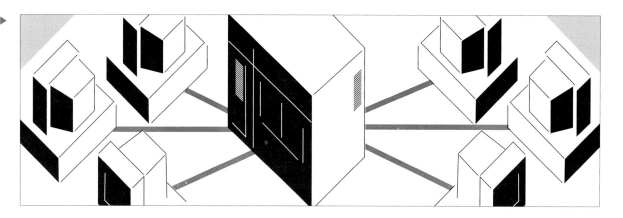

# Connecting networks together

Networks come in all sizes, and most of what you've read so far applies equally to large and small networks. But some aspects of networking aren't encountered until a network needs to expand.

Many networks are really composed of several smaller networks that have been connected together. These individual networks were established independently to meet the different needs of different work groups, but users often find that their independent work groups need to communicate with one another.

In some cases, established networks need to be connected together; in others, a network may need to grow beyond its maximum number of devices or the maximum length of cable; in still others, transmissions may need to span different types of networks. For these and other reasons, organizations need the means to connect networks to each other.

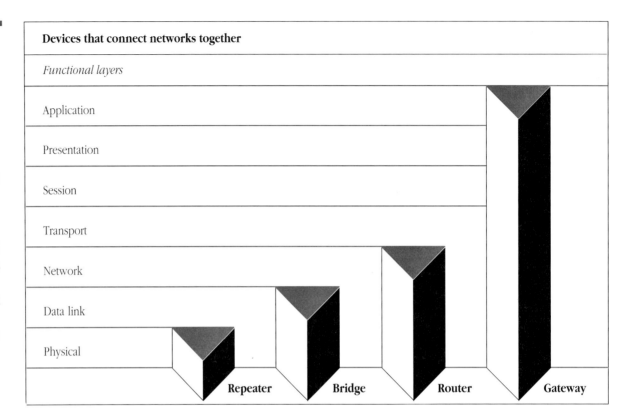

Four kinds of devices are used to connect computer networks:

- Repeaters
- Bridges
- Routers
- Gateways

These connection devices can best be described in terms of the *hierarchy* of network functions presented in Chapter 2. In this hierarchy, you may recall, each layer represents a separate level of network functions.

Network connection devices perform functions that may involve one or more of these layers. The device you pick to do the job depends on what kind of connection services you need.

**Repeaters:** A repeater is used when a network cable needs to be extended beyond its recommended maximum length or maximum number of devices.

A signal becomes weakened as it travels through the network cable. The repeater amplifies and retransmits the signal. The repeater can extend the *distance* covered by a network cable and thereby increase the physical limit to the number of devices that can be connected. For example, adding a repeater to a network with a cable limit of 1,000 feet might increase that limit to 2,000 feet.

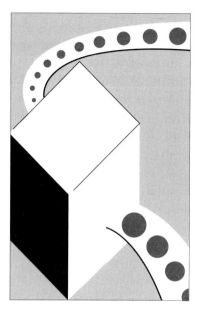

**Bridges:** A bridge's functions involve the first *and* second layers of network protocols.

Using data link protocols, the bridge can read the node address attached to a packet and selectively filter out or transmit the packet depending on its destination.

The networks connected by a bridge remain physically separate entities, governed by their own limits and capacities, but to devices on the rest of the internet they appear as one network.

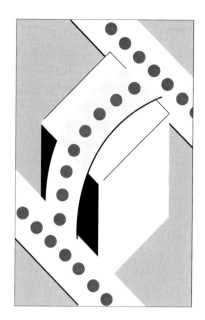

**Routers:** A router is used in internets where more selective decision-making intelligence is required at the point of connection. The router allows connected networks to remain fully independent and to retain separate identities and addresses.

The router is "aware" of the other networks and routers in the internet and can select the most efficient path to the data's intended destination. This ensures faster traffic flow and can automatically provide for detours if a connection is broken along the path.

**Gateways:** Of all connection devices, gateways use the greatest range of networking protocols because they serve as translators between different kinds of network protocol architectures. A gateway is not necessarily used to make a network larger; its primary purpose is to overcome differences between connected networks.

The gateway interprets network-related information in a data transmission, such as addressing and routing instructions, then translates these and the message content into the format of the other protocol, and retransmits the data onto that network.

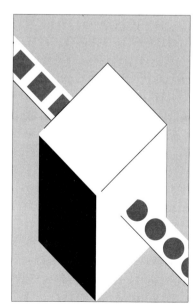

# 4 / Telecommunications in Computer Networks

Telecommunication—from the Greek word *tele*, meaning "at a distance"—is a broad term encompassing the many forms of communication that use long-distance transmission systems rather than direct lines between parties. These include television and radio broadcasting, telephone systems, and satellite communication.

The latter two forms of telecommunication—telephone and satellite systems—play a prominent part in several aspects of computer networking:

- Wide area computer networks
- Public data networks
- Remote access to information services

In the majority of cases, long-distance connections in computer networks use telephone lines as their principal medium. In order to connect a computer to a telephone system, a special device called a modem is required. The modem converts the computer's data into a form that telephone lines can transmit.

## Why we need modems

Computer information, as described in Chapter 2, is transmitted by an electrical signal that corresponds directly to a binary code. This form, called *digital* transmission, is used by all computer systems, but telephone systems use a different form.

Unlike the high/low, either/or signalling method of digital zeros and ones, most telephone systems transmit a signal of continuously varying intensity. This is called *analog* transmission.

Although much telephone equipment is converting to the digital method nowadays, most public phone lines remain analog. A modem is necessary to change—or *modulate*—computer transmissions from digital to analog and back. *Modem* is short for *modulator-demodulator*.

A modem can be a standalone device, usually no larger than a small book, that is connected to a computer and a telephone line, or it can be in the form of a circuit board that is installed inside a computer.

In addition to converting data from digital to analog and back, modems and related software perform many telephone tasks, such as making sure there is a dial tone, dialing phone numbers, listening for connection at the other end, and recognizing busy signals.

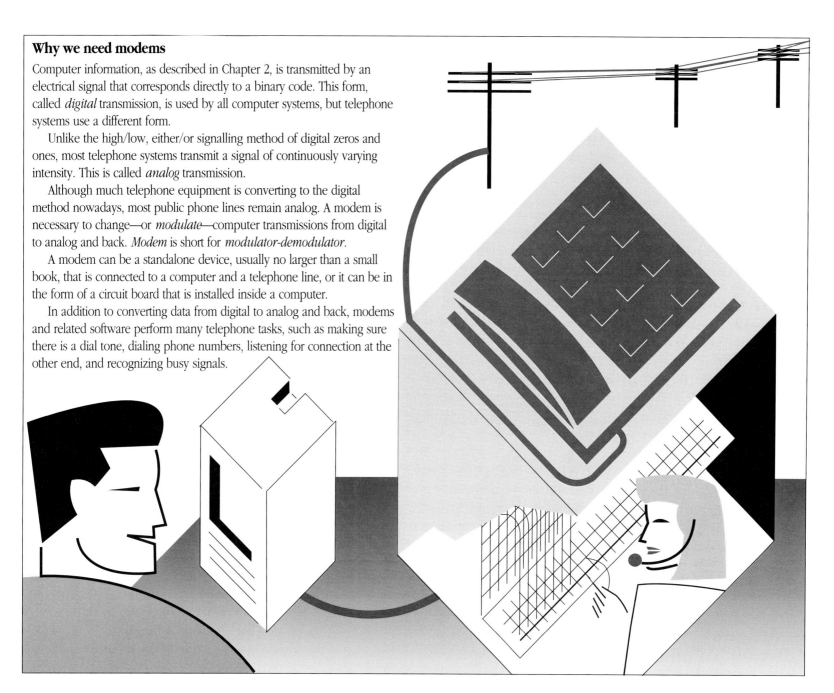

# Wide area networks

Wide area networks, it was noted earlier, generally cover an area that is too large to permit direct local connection between all parts, and involve computers communicating via media such as long-distance telephone lines. Let's elaborate on that now, because some potentially confusing conditions are attached to that definition.

Two computers connected through modems and telephone lines don't necessarily constitute a wide area network. In fact, many companies today own their own local phone equipment, and their private telephone wires may be used to connect computers together into *local area* networks. Such a network might span an office building and connect dozens of computers that share the same wiring and switching equipment used by the company's private telephone network.

However, when these computers use outside lines to access network services that are not connected to the company's private telephone system, they are using the services of a wide area network.

**Telephones used in local area networks**

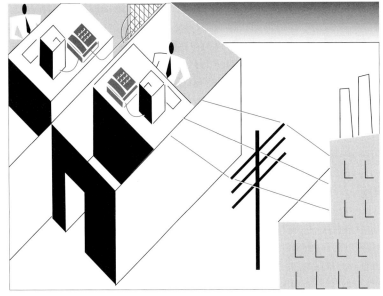

**Telephones used in wide area networks**

## Uses of wide area networks

As illustrated on the facing page, wide area computer networks can be used for two main categories of applications:

- **Private** applications meet the internal communication needs of an organization.
- **Commercial** applications provide information services to the public, usually at a price.

In addition, a prominent use of wide area networks is to connect together government, university, and industry research centers. These institutions use computer networks to share information through a variety of electronic mail and related services.

**Private uses of wide area networks** include activities of an organization that support its internal operations, for example:

- long-distance electronic mail between offices in different cities or countries
- connections between remote departments whose computers must regularly exchange data, such as sales and billing or manufacturing and inventory
- company-wide information systems for employees, such as electronic bulletin board services
- transaction processing between personal computers or terminals and data bases on central computers

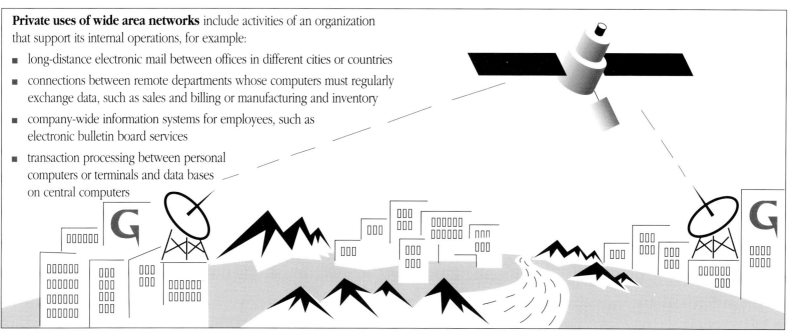

**Commercial uses of wide area networks** include information services provided to the public through a personal computer and modem, or through specialized retail systems, for example:

- credit checking services provided either automatically through point-of-sale terminals or through dial-up services to retailers
- automated teller machines connected to a bank's central customer account database
- reservation systems for airlines, hotels, car rentals, and other services that are connected to a central clearing computer
- dial-up information services like CompuServe, DIALOG, and The Source, which provide a wide range of database files that customers can access and query from computers in their home or business

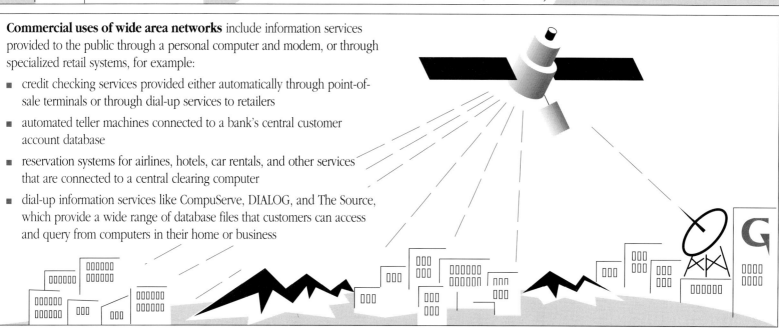

# Public data networks

If you've had the experience of using one of the many on-line information services, you may have noticed that they provide a local telephone number in many cities. You might be in Tucson, Arizona, and dial a local Tucson number, but when your computer connects to the database and accesses the information, it may actually obtain it from a mainframe computer in Paris, France. How does your local connection make that long-distance jump? How does the information service company provide local connections in all those cities?

The answer is that when you dial that local number, your computer connects to a local connection station, called a *node*, in a very large telecommunication network. There are several national and global networks with nodes in hundreds of cities, and the operators of these networks lease time to businesses and information services—like the one in Paris in the example above—so their services can be delivered to a widely distributed user base.

In many countries, these public data networks are government owned and operated, as are most telephone companies. In the U.S., they are privately operated networks.

A key technical distinction of public data networks is that, unlike telephone systems, which transmit information between callers using a method called **circuit-switching,** these networks—in most cases—use a method of routing information called **packet-switching.**

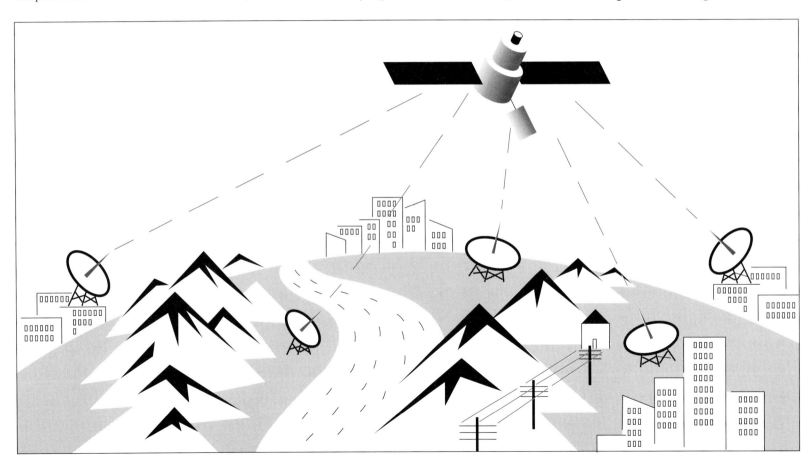

## Circuit switching and packet switching

If that information service in Paris had used the public telephone network to complete your connection, it would have been charged by the telephone company at the long-distance rate between Tucson and Paris for the entire time you remained connected. Even though a connection of this sort is only transmitting a small percentage of the time, the telephone system requires a dedicated circuit between the two points for the duration of the connection.

When you dial out on a public line, the call first reaches a local telephone company office. There, the call is switched to an available circuit that connects to the switching office nearest to the destination being called. For this reason, a telephone system is called a circuit-switched network.

In a packet-switched long-distance network, instead of establishing a dedicated circuit between the caller and destination, the sending node breaks the transmission into packets that are sent independently, and the receiving node at the destination reassembles them. These packets share the network with packets from other transmissions in the most efficient way possible so that the expensive long-distance connections are not left idle for long intervals.

This method enables public data networks to provide long-distance data transmission services at economical rates. Users are charged a price determined by the amount of information—or packets—transmitted during their connection, rather than the length of connection.

Organizations that offer dial-up computer services to the public do not themselves generally have a communication network in place, but use the connection services of a public packet-switched networking company.

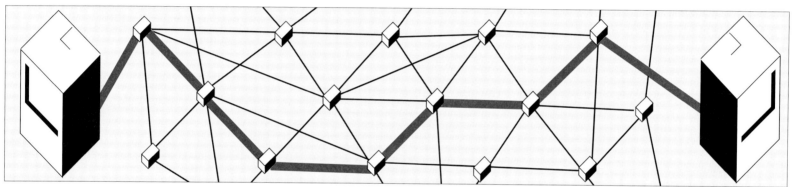

**Circuit Switching**

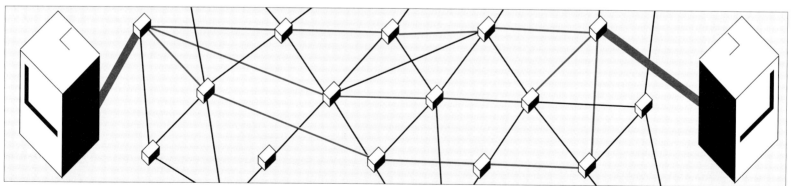

**Packet switching**

## Remote access to information

How does communicating on a wide area network differ from communicating on a local area network? Local area networks usually deliver higher performance. But beyond this, the difference lies in their applications. You turn to a remote computer for information that isn't normally at hand. For example, a researcher might dial up a public database like DIALOG Information Services to obtain bibliographic files, or a sales representative might call her company's inventory computer from the field to check the availability of a product.

But whatever the purpose, a connection to a remote computer can be made in two very different ways: between terminal and host, or computer and computer.

■ A **terminal-to-host** connection doesn't involve any actual processing of information at the user's end. Only a "dumb" terminal—a monitor and keyboard with little or no processing power— and a modem are required. The modem contains the necessary communication software to establish the phone connection. Once you

enter the phone number and are connected to the host, the experience is identical to using a terminal connected locally to that host.

■ In a **computer-to-computer** connection, you can use both local and remote computing power. This means you can not only access information and manipulate it on the host, but you can store it on your own disk, print it on your printer, and display it in formats determined by your own software.

You could, for example, run a program on your personal computer that performs statistical analyses on stock market data and periodically places a call to Dow Jones on-line services to update preselected stock quotations.

There is another fundamental difference between using remote connection methods and being part of a network. While you're connected to a remote computer, you're *using the services* of an existing network (for example, a packet-switched public data network), but you're only a part of that network until you terminate the call. When you use a personal computer on a local network, this computer is an integral part of the network or internet to which it is connected.

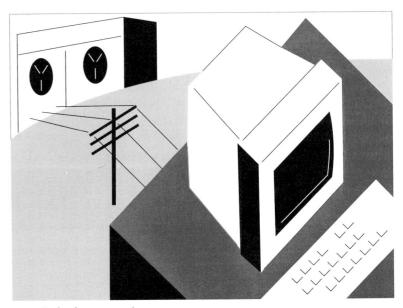

A terminal-to-host connection

A computer-to-computer connection

## The role of communication software

When you connect your computer to a modem and dial up a remote computer, are you now using two computers at once? If not, then which computer are you using?

Often, communication software is designed so that your local computer emulates a "dumb" terminal.

While you are connected to the remote host in this way, your communication software sends all the keystrokes you type out through the modem port to the remote computer. Likewise, everything displayed on your screen is acquired from the remote computer.

Whether or not you retain computing capabilities when connected to a remote computer depends on your own computer's communication software. It needs to have the ability to capture and store the data, and also to format and display it—and if the remote computer's output format is different from its own, it needs to be able to translate the files into some locally intelligible form. Which of these capabilities are present will vary from one communication program to another.

## Preventing unauthorized access

The opportunity for individuals to dial a computer and obtain information vital to organizations and government agencies has raised serious concerns about security. What measures can be taken to allow access to some callers and not to others, or to allow authorized callers to use some parts of a network while restricting others?

*Passwords* are the most common security measure used to protect privacy at all levels—from personal computers to multi-user computers, networks, and remote dial-up installations. Once a password is accepted and the user is admitted, additional levels of password entry may be used to restrict access to other parts of a system or network, or even to prevent the user of an application from getting to a restricted part of that application.

Passwords, however, are often shared among colleagues and friends, making it impossible to fully control access by unauthorized individuals. An added security measure is a *callback* function, wherein the remote computer not only checks the caller's name and password, but also makes sure the source of the call is in fact that user's telephone. Once the caller is identified, the computer hangs up, searches its security file for the preauthorized phone number from which the user may call, calls back, and reconnects.

A *data encryption* scheme may also be used, in which a secret code scrambles the information and makes it readable only by computers using the same code.

Encrypting information in this way—or linking the caller's name, password, and telephone number—greatly reduces the risk of unauthorized access but may not always eliminate it. Network vendors offer security schemes of varying complexity and effectiveness, but security is largely a human issue; the best protection remains for corporate information managers to impose and consistently enforce security measures.

# 5 / Networking in Action

We've looked at computer networks from many sides now: what they are, what they're made of, what makes them work. But if you read in the business pages tomorrow that one computer company is licensing its network protocols to another, you might still be unsure about what that means. Or if you took a walk through the aisles of a computer trade show full of network software and interface gadgetry, you might still be at a loss for the right questions to ask.

What's still missing is how it all works together. Just as you can't learn what a human being is by studying only the parts of the human body, studying the parts and processes of a network won't reveal what networking is really about. Now it's time to look at the *context* of computer networking: how network services are delivered—and how they are used.

# Network services

As we have seen, the devices and applications on a computer network fall into one of three main categories:

- computers
- connecting devices
- network services

The computers are increasingly becoming networked *personal* computers. The connecting devices are the modems, bridges, and various other products that connect the parts of the network.

The network services are the specialized applications of network hardware and software that deliver the benefits of networking to users. Among these, perhaps the most common services are:

- Sharing information
- Sharing network resources
- Communicating with other users

These services are commonly provided to network users through *file servers, print servers*, and *electronic mail*.

## File servers

A prominent and rapidly growing use of networks is to allow users to share information through network **file servers.**

You can use a file server to do the following:

- Make files and applications from your own personal computer available on the server so that other users on the network may access them.

- Copy files and applications to your own personal computer from a file server.

- Access and use files and programs that reside on a server *as if they were located on your own personal computer.*

The kinds of files stored on a server might include documents from a project that several users are working on together, "boilerplate" materials such as form letters or contracts, software that has been licensed for multiple users, or any other information users need to share.

Two kinds of file services may be available on computer networks: *dedicated* file servers and *nondedicated* file service software.

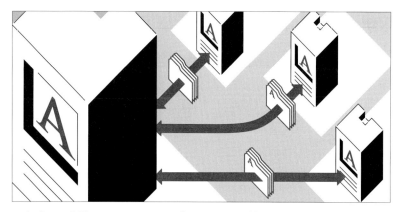

A **dedicated file server** consists of a computer, file server software, and one or more large capacity hard disks. The server computer is connected to the network, and all network users can access its services. Benefits of a dedicated file server include centralized administration, security, and the ability to limit access privileges to specified users.

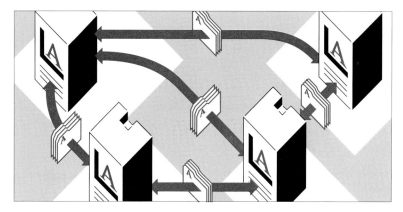

A **nondedicated file server** is a software-based service running on a network user's personal computer. This service is typically set up on several users' hard disks, and allows the users to selectively designate individual files on their own disks for access by other users. Nondedicated file servers provide users the benefit of direct access to each other's files, and the economy of eliminating the dedicated server.

## Print servers

A **print server** is a device that lets multiple network users send files to the same printer simultaneously, regardless of whether or not that printer is currently busy. Rather than having to wait for the printer to become free, users transmit their files to the server and return to other tasks. The server stores the files until the designated printer is available.

Although printer sharing on a network does not require a print server, this service makes printing more efficient. The server consists of special software operating on a dedicated or shared computer. This computer is the device to which a user's computer actually transmits documents intended for printing. The file server software then coordinates printing documents from multiple users.

Two principal benefits are derived from print servers:

■ The server enables users to regain immediate use of their computers after transmitting a document for printing, rather than causing them to wait until printing has completed.

■ Print server software may allow the order of printing to be selected by users, printing either in the order received or giving priority to selected documents.

## Electronic mail

Typical electronic mail applications use either a *mail server* approach or a *direct delivery* approach.

In the server approach to electronic mail, one computer—which may or may not be used for other services—is designated as a mail server. Mail server software is installed on this server computer, and user software is installed on each user's computer.

When any user sends a message to any other, the message is stored on this server in a private "electronic mailbox" for the addressee, who may then retrieve the message from the server at any time.

This is highly efficient because the addressee's computer doesn't need to be turned on or connected at the time of sending. A message sent to multiple users needs to be mailed only once, from the sender to the server, where it is then made available to each addressee.

In the *direct delivery* approach to electronic mail, messages are sent directly from one user node to another. The advantages of this method are the elimination of the need for a server computer and the possibility of more direct "conversations" between users.

However, direct delivery mail systems forfeit the efficiencies of servers described above, and are more complex because each node must have the capacity to directly address all other nodes rather than simply a single server.

# How network services are delivered

The network services described in the preceding sections can be delivered to users by several methods. These methods are characterized by different combinations of hardware and software:

- A dedicated hardware device
- A dedicated server computer
- A multiple-service computer
- A nondedicated service

Note that the first three methods are server-based. Each involves a device that is specially designated for the task. In contrast, the fourth type—a service in a nondedicated computer—requires no central device or server.

**A dedicated hardware device.** ▶
A network service may be provided by a specialized hardware device, such as a shared laser printer, or a "black box" that connects the network to other networks.

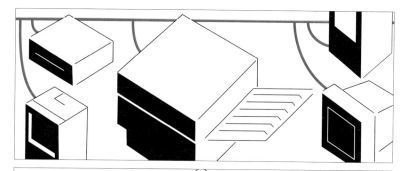

**A dedicated server computer.** ▶
A network service may be provided by a *combination* of a computer and software; for example, a personal computer with a large hard disk that is dedicated as a file server, running file server software and providing shared storage to network users.

**A multiple-service computer.** ▶
Two or more services may be provided concurrently by the same computer. For example, a file server, a print server, and an electronic mail server might all be operating on the same network computer.

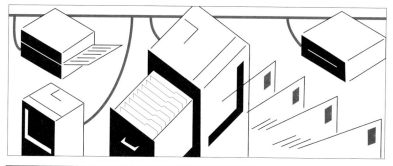

**A nondedicated service.** ▶
A network service can also be provided by special software programs that reside in a network user's own personal computer. For example, nondedicated file server software, when installed in a user's computer, lets other network users access data on that user's hard disk.

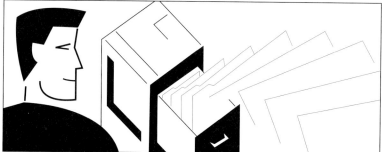

# Commercial services provided by computer networks

Many services of computer networks are available to you *outside* of the workplace. These are *commercial* services—often referred to as dial-up or on-line services—that are made available to consumers through wide area public data networks. You may be using some of these services already and will find others becoming increasingly common.

Such commercial services may be delivered in one of two ways:

- Through your own personal computer (or terminal) and a modem. These tools give you access to a constellation of sources of knowledge, means of communication, and providers of goods.

- Through specialized retail terminals connected to a central data base, such as a bank's computer.

The examples that follow represent some of the many commercial services available.

## Information services

On-line information services are available from private vendors, such as DIALOG Information Services, as well as from many libraries and universities. These sources allow you to dial a central database computer, submit key words to identify your subject of interest, and receive personalized bibliographic lists of reference sources. These lists are produced by computer searches of databases containing thousands or millions of records for books and articles, each indexed by a list of key-word identifiers.

These databases are maintained in vast computer storage facilities connected to mainframe computers that can handle many callers at once. Connections between these database computers and callers' personal computers are generally made via public data networks, although private campus-wide networks provide similar services in some universities.

## Electronic mail

Commercial electronic mail is used for the same purposes as the organization-wide mail systems described earlier. But instead of being limited to members of one organization, the service is made available to the public on a subscription basis.

Each subscriber receives a mail address and can use a personal computer to connect to the network. Once connected, the subscriber can send messages to other subscribers and pick up his or her messages.

The mail system consists of a central computer containing a database of messages. This computer can be accessed from any location by telephone, using the services of a public data network.

Messages in the database are identified using the subscriber's address; for example, a subscriber whose address is JONES116 can dial in and collect all messages for that address. Subscribers are charged for the service on the basis of the number of messages sent and the time connected.

## Bulletin boards

Electronic bulletin board services have been around for many years, in many forms.

Before becoming available through commercial services, these electronic "meeting places" were provided as open message centers in computers connected to many users through local terminals and wide area networks. Such bulletin boards are common in the academic and scientific computing communities.

With the advent of commercial dial-up networks, electronic bulletin boards catering to a variety of special interests have been opened to the public. In contrast to electronic mail messages, which are directed to individual subscriber addresses, bulletin board messages are stored in groups indexed by subject, and may be read by any subscriber to the bulletin-board service.

Subjects may range from job listings, event calendars, or singles registers to political discussions and idea forums.

### Electronic banking

Most people are familiar with one common form of electronic banking services: those provided by automated teller machines, or ATMs. ATM terminals have proliferated to the point of collectively handling millions of transactions per day. Much as with any popular technology, ATMs are now largely taken for granted, and used as naturally as push-button telephones.

Each ATM is a specialized computer terminal connected via a wide area network to its corresponding bank's computerized account databases. There, every transaction is validated and recorded.

Another emerging form of electronic banking services is provided directly to individual customers through personal computers. These computer services include all types of personal banking transactions, such as transferring funds and viewing account balances—although communication networks stop short of being able to dispense currency.

### Credit checking

Credit card purchases are made by the millions each day, and a large number of these involve some form of credit clearance through computerized customer account databases.

To communicate with these computer databases, retailers use one of three methods:

- Person-to-person telephone contact with a database entry clerk at a central clearing computer.

- Electronic credit checking through a specialized card-scanning terminal connected to a central clearing computer via a wide area network.

- Direct connection between an electronic cash register and a credit clearing computer.

With the current advent of debit cards linked directly to consumer checking accounts, connections are also becoming necessary between point-of-sale terminals and bank checking account databases.

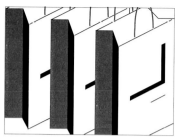

### Home shopping

As recent decades have produced increasing numbers of two-career families with fewer leisure hours for shopping, mail-order selling has become a booming industry. It is a natural extension of this trend that personal computers are now being used to deliver mail order catalogs to consumers' homes.

Through dial-up access to the electronic catalogs of major retailers, consumers are able to peruse listings of thousands of items for personal, household, recreational, or other uses. They may then order these directly by entering credit information.

As with other types of on-line services, computer shopping services are delivered from the central computerized databases of retailers to the personal computers of consumers via public data networks.

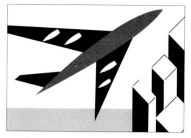

### Airline ticketing

One of the consumer services provided by vendors of on-line services is access to airline schedules and ticket purchasing.

Subscribers to such a service may view airline schedules to determine the most desirable flight to a given destination, and then actually purchase tickets by simply entering identification and credit card information.

The preceding examples represent only the beginning of the trend to deliver consumer services by computer. Commercial applications for networks will become far more widespread as personal computers enter more and more consumer households.

# 6 / Managing the Network

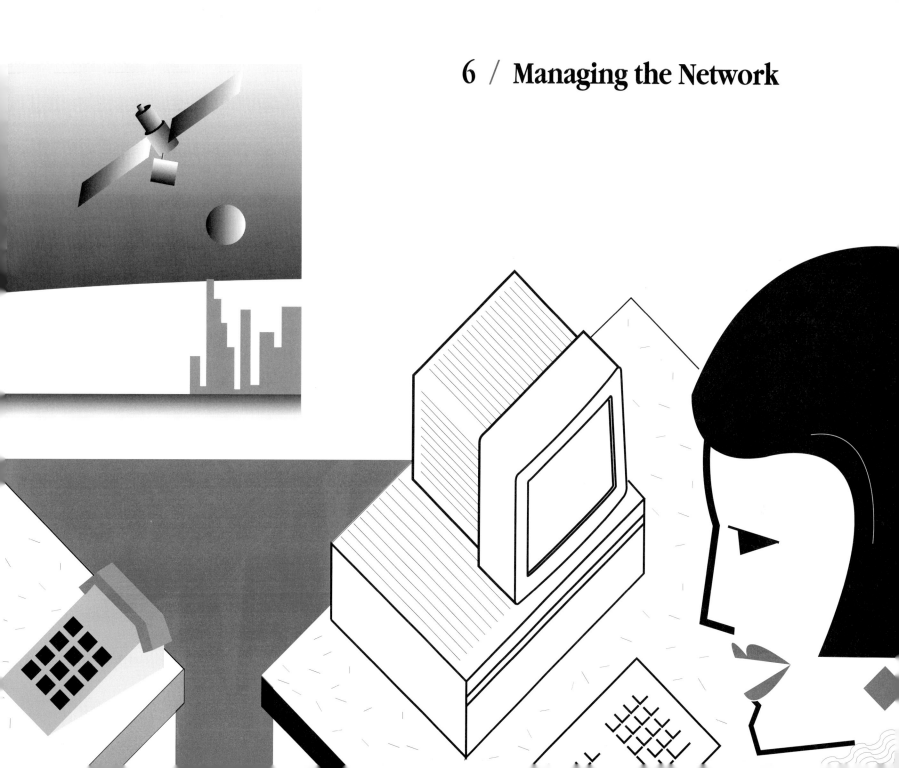

This book was written in the belief that a body of knowledge as vast as the technology of computer networks is best approached with a clear view of the total picture, rather than a detailed analysis of the parts.

Much more can be said—and has been—about each of the subjects discussed here. Future books in this series will cover such subjects as network administration, protocols, and terminology, and will deal with these in greater depth.

This final chapter attempts to leave you with some thoughts about the future: where computer networking appears to be headed, and where you—as a network user—may wish to turn your attention next.

The concerns that are probably greatest in networking today are how to *manage* growing networks and how to *standardize* the flood of new network products and services so that they can be effectively used together. Here are some of the issues that dominate these discussions.

# Network planning

One of the few generalizations that can be made about networks is that they don't stay the same size for very long.

Organizations grow, users want more network services in more places, disparate groups want to connect to one another, and before long a small office network can become a sprawling plexus of cables, modems, routers, and all varieties of connection hardware.

Managing growth—beginning with careful advance planning—has become the key to successful networking. One cannot overemphasize the long-term benefits in both performance and reliability obtained by planning network growth.

The planning issues listed here apply to *ongoing* network growth as well as to new networks.

### Network needs analysis

Some computer networks are set up to serve huge multinational corporations. Others start in a garage office. Whether the organization needs to connect many existing networks or just a few computers and printers, the planning process begins by taking inventory of current network needs.

■ **Communication needs:** The key factors that determine communication needs include the numbers of devices and locations that need to be connected, their geographical separation, and the feasibility of direct or telephone connections.

■ **Network service needs:** This is the user side of the equation: the selection of network services. What are the communication tasks that the network will be used for? Is the network being set up to enable sharing printers and file servers? Will electronic mail play a part, and, if so, will it be local or over long-distance lines? Planning for network services means analyzing the network's possible applications and determining which will benefit users most.

### Market evaluation

Once the organization's networking needs have been assessed, network planning turns to evaluating alternative solutions and picking the ones that fit best. It's important to note that these decisions involve more than just selecting hardware and software.

■ **Vendor analysis:** This includes evaluating the product offerings of different companies and the completeness of their product lines, performing cost comparisons, finding out about vendor service organizations, and examining all factors that will enter into the vendor-client relationship.

■ **Integration of network technologies:** Network planners must evaluate and compare the *flexibility* of available network systems—do they enable computers and network products to be connected to others that use different communication methods?

### Preparation for growth

Assessing an organization's current network needs helps to define its *minimum* requirements—but cannot produce its total network planning strategy. Accounting for growth is a critical element of that strategy. By anticipating the way a network will evolve, the organization can help that evolution to be efficient and responsive to users' needs—rather than be forced into a reactive role, forever playing catch up to connect new devices and networks.

■ **Projected expansion:** One aspect of network evolution is strictly quantitative; it deals with projecting the increase in the numbers of users, computers, and services and the anticipated level of use.

■ **Projected new services and diversification:** The other aspect of a network's evolution depends on the rapidly *changing* industry environment—and the corresponding changes in network services and networking standards that may occur. Planning flexible network systems that support multiple standard protocols can help to keep up with evolving technologies.

## The physical layout

An important aspect of preparing for the future involves the actual physical network plan. The topological design of the network's layout will play an important role in determining how easily you can add new network devices and connect additional networks—while at the same time keeping communication between all points on the network as fast and direct as possible.

Successful planning for network growth requires careful topological design. As an example, a growing internet can be designed like a well-balanced tree, in which each individual network is connected to one of the main branches so that information traveling between any two points on the internet crosses as few networks as possible. This strategy not only improves network performance but makes for a flexible internet in which changes are least disruptive to users.

**A poorly planned, overly complex internet**

**A well-balanced, more manageable internet**

# Network management and administration

Because a network's needs for growth, change, and maintenance are continuous, it's often necessary for responsibility and accountability to be concentrated in one individual or group. As networks proliferate in organizations, the role of the network manager in planning and controlling communication networks is taking center stage among the lifeline support functions of the organization.

## Network administration

In smaller networks, responsibilities for planning the network and managing day-to-day network operations rest with the same person. In larger organizations, however, a central planning group may oversee major network management issues, while local network administration is decentralized. In this way, on-location, individual attention can be paid to networks that are geographically dispersed.

*Network administrators* are individuals responsible for the day-to-day functions of computer networks, including such matters as connecting computers and other devices, helping users with network problems, managing security and access to the network, and maintaining, monitoring, and troubleshooting the network.

■ **Installation:** An administrator's job may involve installing or moving network cables, installing and setting up connecting devices such as bridges and routers, installing and setting up network servers and software, and connecting or moving personal computers for users.

■ **Network management tools:** The job of maintaining a computer network is made easier by a wide range of network management tools. These are hardware and software products that provide network managers and administrators with valuable information and services. Network management tools can report on the number, location, and status of devices connected to the network, identify a wide variety of problem conditions, monitor network performance, and monitor, analyze, and report on the level and nature of activity on various parts of the network.

■ **Maintenance and trouble-shooting:** A large portion of network administration is devoted to maintaining a smoothly functioning network. The network administrator, with the help of network management tools, is responsible for the physical and functional integrity of the network: If a user should inadvertently disconnect a segment of cable, it's up to the administrator to discover and correct the situation. If network performance slows down as the result of some mysterious cause, the administrator must locate and correct the problem.

The ultimate objective of all network administration is providing network users with the highest possible network performance—with the fewest possible disruptions in their network services.

# What multiple computer vendors mean to networking

In the computer industry, the manufacturer of a brand of computers or networks is known as a "vendor." Apple, IBM, and Digital Equipment Corporation are all vendors.

Most organizations that use computers have acquired those computers over a period of years, purchasing hardware and software from multiple vendors. When the time comes to connect users together, companies cannot be expected to replace all these dissimilar computers.

To address this issue of network integration, vendors have been moving to develop and support standards, and to create networking solutions that work with diverse computers. The new term *interoperability* implies reaching beyond mere compatibility to the point where equipment from different vendors can be used interchangeably on each other's networks. Increasingly, users are demanding this kind of versatility from network vendors.

Several strategies exist to achieve interoperability among computers and networks from different vendors.

■ **Special interface devices,** as described in Chapter 3, can be installed into computers to make them compatible with certain networks. Interface devices are usually circuit boards with transceivers and ports that can connect to a "foreign" network system and run software that implements the protocols of that network system.

For example, Apple's LocalTalk-PC interface card enables IBM personal computers to be directly connected to Apple's LocalTalk network and to communicate, using special software, with AppleShare file servers.

■ **Protocol support.** When the protocols of one vendor's network are implemented in products from other vendors, more products become available for that network.

For example, different AppleTalk protocols exist for managing different network functions, such as network access, file service, and printer access. A vendor wanting its computers to be able to connect to AppleTalk networks would need to comply with AppleTalk's protocols

that manage connection, and design these into its network software. If, in addition, the vendor wanted its computers to work with AppleShare® file servers, it would also have to build AppleTalk Filing Protocol capabilities into its products, and so on for other networking functions.

■ **Terminal emulation software** allows a personal computer to *emulate*, or transmit in the format of, a given computer terminal.

Minicomputer and mainframe computer programs normally expect input from users in a specific format generated by that computer's terminals. The Digital VT series and IBM 3270 series of terminals are common examples.

If networked personal computers are to be connected to such a host computer, they need emulation software to transmit data in the format that the host programs expect. The users' computers can then serve double duty as terminals to the host and independent personal computers.

The user's benefit in substituting a personal computer for a terminal is that the computer provides both desktop computing power and host communication capability. The terminal, on the other hand, is strictly an input/output device to the host.

■ **Gateways between networks with dissimilar protocols,** as described in Chapter 3, serve as protocol *translators* to connect networks that use different communication standards.

■ **Standards** are specifications for network protocols that can be used by different vendors so that their products work together. Network standards are discussed in detail on page 66.

# Integrating network technologies

The variety of networking services and interconnection methods described in this chapter may suggest the breadth and diversity of the marketplace for network products. Compatibility is needed not only in connecting one computer to another or one vendor's network to another's, but also in mixing and matching dissimilar media, topologies, and network protocols.

The freedom of choice that organizations have exercised in purchasing computers and network products has created an ever-growing range of interconnection needs. This freedom of choice must continue because it guarantees the best match to individual user needs. Yet users demand simple solutions. However complex the network, internetworking products must present the user with a simple, uniform interface to network products and services—an interface that makes the network transparent.

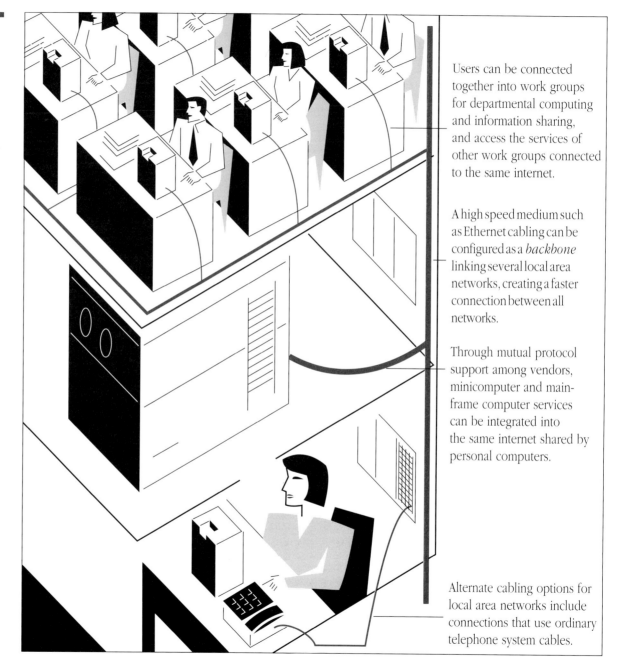

Users can be connected together into work groups for departmental computing and information sharing, and access the services of other work groups connected to the same internet.

A high speed medium such as Ethernet cabling can be configured as a *backbone* linking several local area networks, creating a faster connection between all networks.

Through mutual protocol support among vendors, minicomputer and main-frame computer services can be integrated into the same internet shared by personal computers.

Alternate cabling options for local area networks include connections that use ordinary telephone system cables.

# Network standards

One response from both vendors and users to the proliferation of dissimilar networks has been to push for more standards among networking products.

A **standard** is a set of specifications for designing software or hardware that is developed by one vendor, a group of vendors, or an official standards organization. By observing standard specifications, a vendor can produce a product that works compatibly with others using the same standard.

A standard may cover a *range* of protocols and may be adopted in whole or in part. If a product uses a standard specification, it can communicate with other products that use this standard, but only at the level of functionality pertaining to that standard. For example, if two computers support the same media and connection standards, they can both transmit data on the same media, but if their formats for addressing are different, they will be unable to communicate with each other.

There are three principal ways that standards for networking protocols come into existence. Each is described here, followed by a few current examples.

## Vendor-developed standards

Sometimes, a protocol architecture designed by an individual vendor is adopted by others who wish to connect their products to that vendor's products. Such vendor-developed protocols can become *de facto* standards, meaning that a community of independent vendors recognizes their importance and complies with their specifications.

- **AppleTalk** protocols have been adopted by many vendors of computers and other network products. Connectivity products from Apple and other vendors enable AppleTalk networks to be integrated with other network systems, making AppleTalk services available on a variety of networks and computers.

- **Systems Network Architecture,** or **SNA**, is an architecture developed by IBM for communication among the company's computers and network products connected to them. Many SNA-compatible products from a variety of vendors are being marketed today.

## Industry standards

Industry standards are standards that have been jointly developed and supported by an alliance of industry organizations, whose members may represent vendors, universities, and government.

In contrast with a vendor-developed standard, which is focused on resolving particular user needs, an industry standard is generally fueled by the need to promote coherence in the industry.

- **Ethernet** is a standard developed jointly by Digital Equipment Corporation, Xerox, and Intel, which specifies protocols for connection and high speed transmission in local area networks.

- **TCP/IP** (Transmission Control Protocol/Internet Protocol) is the networking protocol standard most widely used in U.S. government and university internets. It is broadly supported among major industrial contractors and university research centers that communicate with government agencies.

## International standards

Standards are often developed by internationally sanctioned committees whose primary mission is to help define specifications for communication products. Their challenge is to develop standards that are flexible enough to be adapted in different ways by different vendors—but rigid enough to ensure that these adaptations produce networks that work together.

- **X.25** is a standard recommended by the international communications committee known as the CCITT. This standard specifies an interface for connecting computers to a packet-switched network.

- **X.400** is a recommendation of the CCITT that is gaining acceptance as the international standard for electronic mail.

The seven-layer OSI reference model of the International Standards Organization, discussed earlier, is a *model*—not a standard. Its modular form helps to represent protocol functions in an orderly way, but does not assure compatibility among networks that observe the model. The ISO has also published many different standards that explicitly specify protocols corresponding to certain layers of the OSI model.

Work continues in the industry to develop standards that address a more complete range of networking technologies and applications and that reach across international boundaries. Multiple standards, like different languages, will continue to coexist, driven by different user needs and applications. Evolving network technologies must successfully mask these differences to present users with well-integrated network interfaces.

## ISDN—A look at wide area networking to come

Integrated Services Digital Network (ISDN) is an evolving set of standards for unifying a broad range of voice, data, text, and image communication services in one *digital* wide area network.

The ultimate concept of ISDN is for a worldwide public telecommunications network provided by telephone companies, integrated with equipment and services provided by private vendors, presenting a broad selection of services to the end user through standard network interfaces.

In addition to the obvious benefits of integrating data communication with voice and pictures, the transmission quality and performance of a fully digital network will be higher than what's available with current methods. Modems and the relatively slow data transfer rates now associated with telephone transmission could become a thing of the past, and the potential gains in productivity of integrated information services will be tremendous.

Naturally, a plan to convert communication on a global scale can only be implemented gradually. The architecture and technical specifications of ISDN are still evolving, and telecommunications agencies face many technical and business obstacles before such a conversion can be completed. However, by the mid-1990s, users can expect to see the impact of ISDN in communication services offered to government, business, education, and—ultimately—to the home.

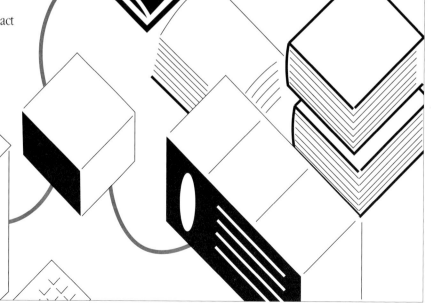

# The future

Had this book been written five years ago, it would have been a very different book. Five years into the future, the appearance and methods of computer networking will be just as different again. This book has tried to answer the question "What is a computer network today?"

It's important to remember this ongoing evolution when defining any aspect of computer technology. The natural and physical sciences may develop rapidly as well, but their ground rules change at a slower rate. Trees, planets, and people remain the same even as our knowledge about them evolves. In contrast, computer networking technology is among the most recent and most dynamic products of human industry, and its ground rules are still being formed and continually reinvented.

If, for example, wireless transmission methods such as infrared and microwave continue to gain prominence in the networking industry, fundamental definitions of such terms as media, network connections, and topologies will change radically. As ISDN (see preceding page) becomes a reality, telecommunication technologies will become more difficult to distinguish from computer network technologies.

Experience has shown that reports of the limits of computing capabilities—such as processing or transmission speeds, or storage capacities—become obsolete almost as soon as they appear in print. Doubtlessly, the future will bring levels of performance and seamless communication between different kinds of systems, media, and applications that today might be considered science fiction.

Through all this change, however, one thing remains constant. Computer networking continues to serve people by increasing their power to learn, to work, and to communicate.

# Epilogue

## A Conversation With Donald P. Casey

*Vice President of Networking and Communications, Apple Computer, Inc.*

**If we stop to consider the impact that computer technology has had on our lives, it's a bit awesome to think that that's only the beginning—that computer networking now stands to deliver even more revolutionary services to individuals. How can we put into perspective the potential of networking in terms of where the industry stands today?**

The technology of networking has been evolving *with* the technology of computers. It's an extension of the same technology, in that it brings us to a new age where it is reasonable to think about the movement of vast amounts of data—among people sitting in front of personal computers.

The evolution of computer technology has led to *personal* computers that are now capable of requesting, receiving, and processing information from a variety of sources around the world. So we have networking technology that can deliver the information, and personal computers now powerful enough to do nearly anything we want to do with that information.

But what are the issues that stand in our way? One is usability. There are more acronyms per square inch in networking and communications than in any other area of data processing. We cannot allow that to get in the way of the user doing what he or she wants to do, which is to communicate. Somehow our solutions have to mask the underlying complexity of the network and deliver what the user wants—not a description of a set of wires or a topology, but easy access to people and information.

The second issue is broad-based availability of information. We have to strongly encourage the movement of many vendors of computer systems toward adequate, efficient, and complete standards so that more people with different systems can communicate with one another.

Finally, we must look to the continued evolution of both technologies. Networks must continue to deliver better speed and better quality at affordable prices, and computer technology needs to continue to evolve not only in terms of power, but in terms of enhancing the personal computer *experience*.

**What would you say have been the most interesting changes in networking you've seen in recent years?**

The movement of power to the desktop and the increasing interest in peer–to–peer networking, in fact the user's *requirement* for peer–to–peer networking.

**But as so many new network products emerge, aren't people being overwhelmed by the number of different technologies and protocols? In what way is the industry moving to simplify that situation for the user and how long might it take?**

I think the industry is driven largely by customers—which is good—and is working, together with several standards bodies and associations, to agree upon communications protocols. Some of these agreements are now being reached. We have international protocols to some degree; X.25 and X.400 are two good examples; ISDN will be another.

But what the industry is doing to standardize networking for users is only a first step. The real key is to focus *not* on the communications protocols, but on what the person sitting in front of the personal computer wants to *do*. I believe we need to design and develop products from the user's viewpoint into the network—not from the network out. We need to make the complex technology of the network transparent to the user.

As to *when* we will get to a standard networking environment, we have implementations now, and they will become increasingly important over time, but I still believe that, due to the investments that customers have made, the existing networks and network architectures will be around for a long time.

**Does that translate into the continued evolution of many parallel standards?**

Yes, I think we will always see parallel developments of proprietary networking architectures from different vendors, but at the same time we will see the evolution of international standards. Both will continue.

**Working closely with many of Apple's largest customers, you must be especially sensitive to multivendor customers' needs. In what ways is networking evolving to meet the needs of the multivendor customer environment?**

There are two ways, and they are concurrent. One, as I said, is the implementation of common standard protocols by different vendors, which will certainly help. Second, some vendors—particularly Apple—because of the needs and investments of their customer base, are implementing the means to work with proprietary protocols of other vendors.

A good example of this second category is what Apple is doing with its own proprietary network system, AppleTalk. Because AppleTalk now reaches such a large customer base, the means have been developed to use AppleTalk on a long list of non-Apple platforms, such as MS-DOS, UNIX®, and VAX/VMS. In order to provide our customers with what they tell us they want, we must work closely with other vendors, such as Digital, and support other proprietary architectures, such as IBM's SNA.

**What network services are showing themselves to be most important to the business customer?**

First, connectivity support, which allows the customer to enhance the *value* of his current network investment. Second, access to information from a personal computer.

Customers are noticing that the use of some personal computers by their employees is enhancing the creativity—and therefore the productivity and effectiveness—of their people. Therefore, the most valuable things that a network can do is to allow those same people, first, to connect to additional computing resources and, second, to utilize additional information so that their insights can be better informed and more valuable to the corporation.

**What do you feel are the most important networking needs that are not yet being met in the marketplace?**

I'd say that we have the *beginnings* of the implementation of standard protocols, but we're not there yet. From an international perspective we are beginning to see ISDN, but we're not there yet either. What we're aiming for is a pervasive implementation of standard protocols as well as expanded standards to enable us to access information in any form—data, text, voice, graphics, and so on—on any media, including magnetic tapes and optical disks, at a high transmission speed.

**How will we know when we are there?**

When you can order, from any vendor, a personal computer, a mainframe, and a minicomputer and not have to ask, first, "Can they communicate?" and, second, "Can I afford to have them communicate?" Then we are there.

**What would you say to the computer user who is intrigued by all this talk of a networking revolution but doesn't see what's in it for him or her?**

I'd say, "Think about the time in your life when you discovered the library and observed that, 'Gee, there's a lot of information there.' Now think about whether you would like access to all of the information in a library when you're sitting in front of your personal computer. If the answer is "yes," then networking and the evolution of this technology are important to you."

To the business user, I would ask, "What if you could communicate with anyone in your organization, or anyone in the world, through your personal computer? What if you could access and use your corporate information databases at any time from anywhere in the world?"

That's what standards and affordable communications technology offer over the long haul. To be able to locate and talk to anyone in the world. Of course, *talk* is the wrong metaphor because we can do that over our telephone system. But when we think of the telephone system, it is a global system we are familiar with, that we can describe and understand. A personal computer system tends to be a much more local thing, not a worldwide thing. Wouldn't it be interesting if some day we had a *personal* computer system that was also worldwide? If what comes to your mind when someone says "telephone system" today is the same thing that would come to your mind when someone said "computer system" or "network?" Then, we will have arrived. The potential is there.

**How would you recommend that a user proceed to learn more about networks and their services after reading this book?**

If I wanted to get a first taste for what networking can offer, then I would subscribe to one of the information services and start accessing the vast amount of information that's available on every desktop—whether that desk happens to be at work or at home. In that process, I may also be exposed to, and, one hopes, learn about, additional services such as electronic mail—the ability to send text information to one or many people instantly.

You learn two things: One is that you like it; access to new information in a convenient, timely manner is wonderful. The second is that it's not *yet* as easy as you'd like it to be or as inexpensive as you'd like it to be.

**Will that change soon? What's the most promising development network users can look forward to in coming years?**

The emergence of networks in which the technology is invisible to the user, networks that a user simply plugs into and uses without worrying about their inner workings.

We already have a wonderful personal computer that can provide users with a great creative experience. By fueling the evolution of communication standards, we will achieve easier-to-use, higher-speed, more affordable networks that enable us to *expand* that computer experience—to provide simple access to information and people around the world.

# Glossary

**access method**—the rules that manage how all the computers and other devices on a network can send information through the same physical medium in an orderly fashion.

**addressing**—a scheme, determined by network protocols, for identifying the sending device and destination device for any given item of information traveling on a network.

**application** (usually application program)—software that a user interacts with, or uses. Examples of applications are word processing programs, spreadsheet programs, and electronic mail programs.

**architecture**—the design plan of a network that determines how the network's components function together.

**bandwidth**—the range of transmission frequencies that a network can use. The greater the bandwidth, the greater the amount of information that can travel on the network at one time.

**baseband**—a transmission method in which a network uses its entire transmission frequency range to send a single communication or signal. Contrast with **broadband.**

**bridge**—a device that links similar networks to each other to allow devices on one network to transmit data to devices on another. Compare with **gateway, repeater,** and **router.**

**broadband**—a transmission method in which the network's range of transmission frequencies is divided into separate channels and each channel is used to send a different signal. Broadband transmission is often used to send signals of different kinds simultaneously, such as voice and data. Contrast with **baseband.**

**bus topology**—a layout scheme in which devices on a network are connected along the length of a main cable, or *bus*, rather than in a daisy chain or a loop.

**carrier sensing**—an **access method,** often referred to by the acronym CSMA, for *carrier sense, multiple access.* According to this method, computers check the network medium to see if it is being used and wait for it to be free before transmitting.

**circuit switching**—a transmission method in which the path, or circuit, along the network between the sending and receiving devices is dedicated to transmitting data only between these two devices. Contrast with **packet switching.**

**coaxial cable**—one type of media used in local area networks. Consists of a central wire surrounded by a layer of insulation, a conductive metal shield, and an outer insulator.

**electronic mail**—a network service that enables users to send and receive messages via computer.

**fiber optic cable**—see **optical fiber.**

**file server**—a network device, usually consisting of a computer and one or more large capacity disks, on which network users can store files and applications in order to share them.

**formatting**—the process by which information is arranged into **packets,** or prepared for transmission on a network. Includes the addition of sender and destination addresses, and other transmission control information.

**gateway**—a device that connects networks that use different protocols. In effect, it translates between the protocols so that devices on the connected networks can exchange data.

**host computer**—a multi-user computer, such as a minicomputer or mainframe, that serves as a central processing unit for a number of terminals.

**interface**—1) The point where two elements of computer or network architecture meet. The interface can be between hardware elements, software elements, or both. 2) *User interface*—the presentation style of the elements of software and hardware that a user interacts with.

**internet**—a network made up of two or more interconnected local area or wide area networks.

**ISO/OSI model**—see **OSI model.**

**LAN**—**local area network.**

**local area network**—computers and shared devices connected to the same network medium in a limited area, usually a single building. Compare with **wide area network.**

**mainframe**—a large computer, generally with a high level of processing power and the capacity to support many users at once.

**media**—the physical conductor of network transmissions, including electrical or optical fiber cables.

**minicomputer**—a multi-user computer, generally with more power than a personal computer yet not as large as a mainframe.

**modem**—a device used to convert computer data into a form that can travel over telephone lines; abbreviation of *modulator/demodulator.*

**multiplexing**—transmitting signals from multiple sources through a single medium.

**name**—the name presented to users of a network to identify a given network service.

**network device**—a computer, printer, modem, terminal, or any other physical entity connected to a network.

**network system**—a family of network components that work together because they observe compatible methods of communication.

**node**—any network device that has an address on the network. (Some network devices, such as modems, may be connected to a network but not be nodes themselves.)

**node number**—a number that distinguishes one node from all others on the network.

**OSI model**—the Open Systems Interconnection (OSI) reference model for describing network **protocols,** devised by the International Standards Organization (ISO); divides protocols into seven **layers** to standardize and simplify protocol definitions.

**optical fiber**—a transmission medium that uses light to transmit a signal.

**packet**—a unit of information that has been formatted for transmission on a network. See also **formatting.**

**packet switching**—a transmission method in which each data **packet** in a given transmission is sent independently. The sequence of packets traveling on a packet-switched network at any given time may originate from different senders and be headed for different destinations. Contrast with **circuit switching.**

**peripheral**—a hardware device that is external to the essential circuitry in a computer. A hard disk and a printer are two examples.

**print server**—a computing device that lets multiple network users send files to the same printer simultaneously, regardless of whether that printer is currently busy.

**protocols**—the rules that govern interaction on a network. Protocols determine where, when, how, and in what format information is transmitted.

**repeater**—a device that extends the maximum length of cable in a single network, so that the network can be expanded. Compare with **bridge, gateway,** and **router.**

**ring topology**—a layout scheme in which network devices are connected by the physical medium in a closed loop.

**route**—the path information takes when it is transmitted from one network device to another.

**router**—a device that connects similar networks to each other. A router receives data transmitted from other nodes and retransmits it to its proper destination over the most efficient route; this route may include several routers, each forwarding the data to the next. Compare with **bridge, gateway,** and **repeater.**

**server**—a network device, usually including specialized software, that delivers some kind of a service to network users, such as file or printer sharing.

**service**—a specialized function that a network provides to users, such as file sharing and electronic mail.

**standard**—a set of specifications for designing hardware or software that is recognized by multiple vendors, an official standards organization, or both.

**star topology**—a layout scheme in which network devices are arranged so that all are connected to a central controlling device.

**terminal**—a keyboard and display screen through which users can access a **host computer.**

**terminal emulation**—software that enables a personal computer to communicate with a **host computer** by transmitting in the form used by the host's terminals.

**transceiver**—a computer's hardware mechanism through which network transmissions are sent and received.

**token passing**—an **access method** according to which devices on a network pass a special sequence of bits, known as the "token," from one device to the next. A device can only transmit data on the network if it is in possession of the token.

**topology**—the physical layout of a network.

**traffic**—transmissions traveling across a network.

**twisted pair cable**—a common, relatively low-cost network cable that consists of two insulated wires twisted about each other.

**WAN—wide area network.**

**wide area network**—computers and/or networks connected to each other using long distance communication methods, such as telephone lines and satellites. Compare with **local area network.**

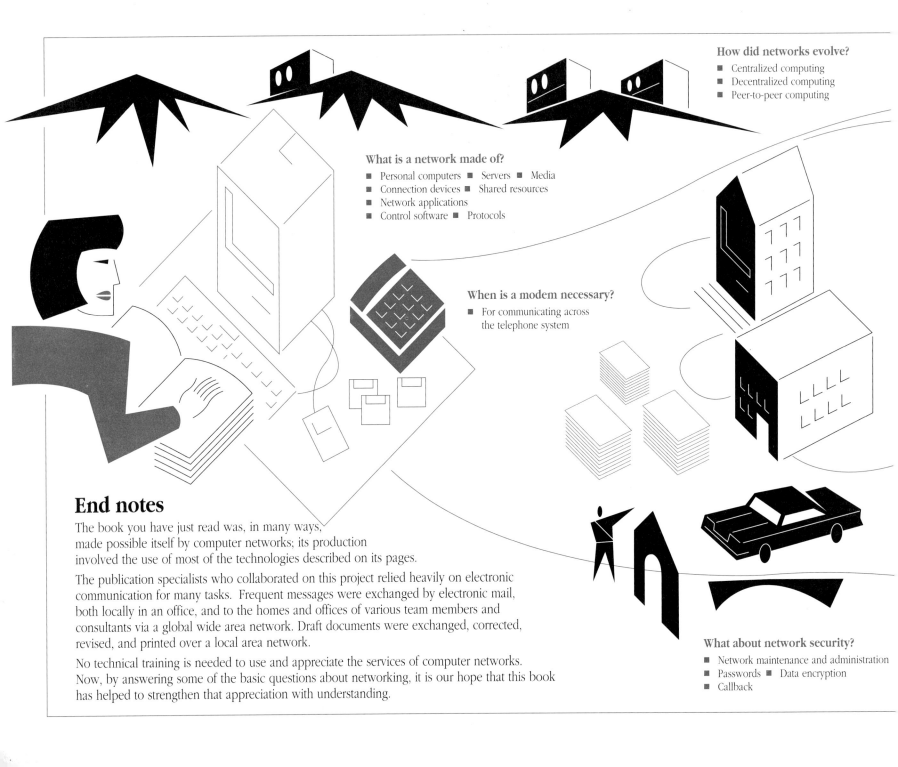

**How did networks evolve?**
- Centralized computing
- Decentralized computing
- Peer-to-peer computing

**What is a network made of?**
- Personal computers ■ Servers ■ Media
- Connection devices ■ Shared resources
- Network applications
- Control software ■ Protocols

**When is a modem necessary?**
- For communicating across the telephone system

# End notes

The book you have just read was, in many ways, made possible itself by computer networks; its production involved the use of most of the technologies described on its pages.

The publication specialists who collaborated on this project relied heavily on electronic communication for many tasks. Frequent messages were exchanged by electronic mail, both locally in an office, and to the homes and offices of various team members and consultants via a global wide area network. Draft documents were exchanged, corrected, revised, and printed over a local area network.

No technical training is needed to use and appreciate the services of computer networks. Now, by answering some of the basic questions about networking, it is our hope that this book has helped to strengthen that appreciation with understanding.

**What about network security?**
- Network maintenance and administration
- Passwords ■ Data encryption
- Callback

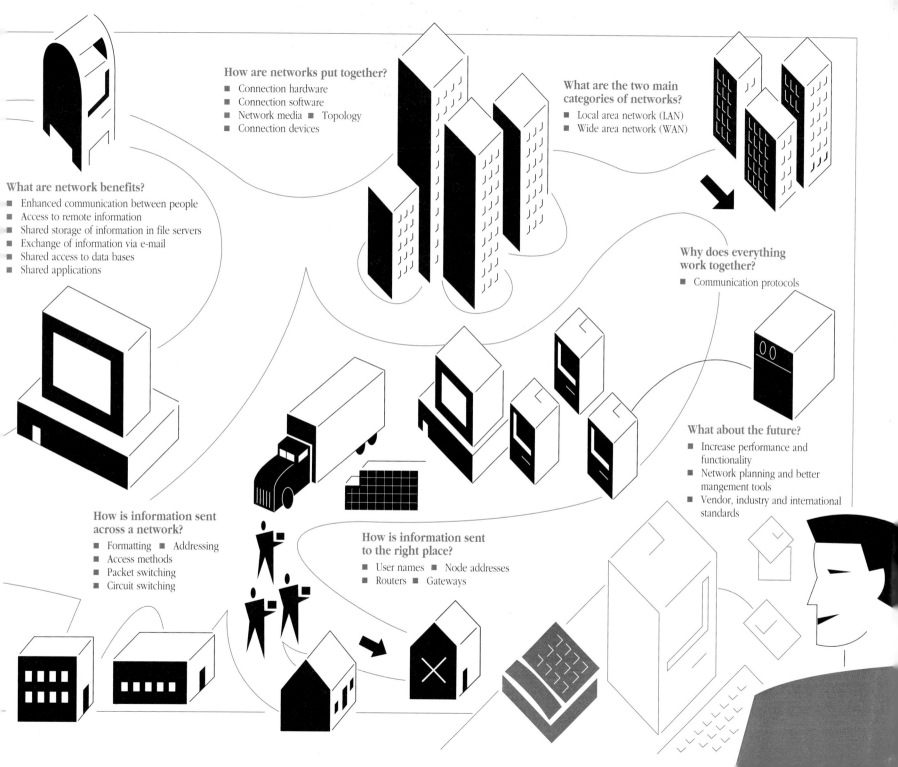

**How are networks put together?**
- Connection hardware
- Connection software
- Network media ■ Topology
- Connection devices

**What are the two main categories of networks?**
- Local area network (LAN)
- Wide area network (WAN)

**What are network benefits?**
- Enhanced communication between people
- Access to remote information
- Shared storage of information in file servers
- Exchange of information via e-mail
- Shared access to data bases
- Shared applications

**Why does everything work together?**
- Communication protocols

**What about the future?**
- Increase performance and functionality
- Network planning and better mangement tools
- Vendor, industry and international standards

**How is information sent across a network?**
- Formatting ■ Addressing
- Access methods
- Packet switching
- Circuit switching

**How is information sent to the right place?**
- User names ■ Node addresses
- Routers ■ Gateways

# Colophon

*Understanding Computer Networks* was written, edited, illustrated, and produced on the Apple® Macintosh® family of computers using Microsoft Word, Aldus PageMaker, and Adobe Illustrator 88. Proof pages were generated on the Apple LaserWriter® family of printers and a Varityper VT600, accessed via an AppleTalk network. Final composition was generated on a Linotronic 300 phototypesetter.

Text and display type are Apple's corporate font, a condensed version of Garamond. ITC Zapf Dingbats are used for miscellaneous elements.